MW01041435

PARTNER'S RECOVERY GUIDE

---

100 EMPOWERING EXERCISES

Douglas Weiss, Ph.D.

© by Douglas W. Weiss, Ph.D.
P.O. Box 16716
Fort Worth, TX 76162-0716
All rights reserved. First Edition 1997, Second Edition 2000
Printed in the United States of America
No portion of this publication may be reproduced
in any manner without the written permission of the publisher
ISBN #1-881292-15-0

TABLE OF CONTENTS

PART TWO: PERSONAL GROWTH TECHNIQUES

APPENDIX

INTRODUCTION

Partner's Recovery Guide has been written for partner's of sex addicts desiring techniques to assist them through their recovery. As a therapist, researcher, author, and lecturer on the subject of sexual addiction, I have counseled many partners of sex addicts both in my outpatient office in Fort Worth, Texas and nationwide through telephone counseling. I have compiled these exercises and principles which have successfully helped many partners of sex addicts to begin and maintain their own personal recovery from the effects of their partner's sexual addiction.

This book is laid out in a progressive chronological order for the partner's of sex addicts recovery. The journey of recovery teaches us "first things first." I encourage you not to pick and choose which exercises you will or will not do but rather receive from each exercise the insight it has to offer after you complete the exercise.

This book can most certainly be used in conjunction with therapy or as part of 12 step relationships you may develop along the journey to recovery. My hope is that you receive the precious gift of recovery and maintain it the rest of your life for your benefit and for the benefit of your partner and/or family.

If we can be of any service along your way, feel free to write to Heart to Heart Counseling Center, P.O. Box 16716, Fort Worth, TX, 76162-0716, or call 817-377-HART (4278). Some of our products at Heart to Heart Counseling Centers include books, videos, workbooks and cassettes on sexual addiction and co-sex addiction. Services provided are telephone and in-office counseling and 3-Day Intensive Workshops. We are also on the World Wide Web at **www.sexaddict.com** providing the largest weekly newsletter for sex addicts and their partners. For a more in-depth listing of services, see the appendix of this book. We look forward to helping you.

Heart to Heart Counseling Centers
P.O. Box 16716
Fort Worth, TX 76162-0716
817-377-4278

PART ONE: BEGINNING TECHNIQUES

EMPOWERMENT EXERCISE #1

DAILY TIME FOR RECOVERY

Recovery, especially from living with a sex addict, will probably be one the hardest undertakings of your life. Recovery is hard work and more importantly, it is consistent work. We will, over the course of this book, be dealing with many issues some of which may be difficult to face. Having a regular time committed to your personal recovery will help you to not put off the hard stuff till later (whenever that is!). The step work, calls, meetings etc. will take some time. So, take some time to make some time. The people who do this are more likely to make greater progress than those who do it when they feel like it.

In light of this, you are going to need time daily to do the many exercises this book will expose you to. These exercises have been proven to work but only if you take the time to do them. This is consistent with the fact that in most areas of life, what you put in to something, is also what you get out. So, whether you need to get a Day Timer calendar or just sit down and have a talk with yourself or your partner, try to come up with at least 15-30 minutes daily in order to work on your recovery from living with a sex addict. This 15-30 minutes daily will make a big difference in how long it will take you to experience recovery. This of course is not the total amount of time you will need as we will discuss later about attending 12 step support groups. Scheduling these meetings in your calendar will also be very important part of your recovery!

EMPOWERMENT EXERCISE #2

EARLY PRAYER

I have not talked to many partners of sex addicts who have not prayed at one time or another in their life. Their prayers consisted of "Oh God, I don't know what is wrong here!" or "If he is cheating on me, let me know" or "Please help him stop...fix him, make him better." Interesting enough, God does hear these prayers and for some, these prayers have been answered although not the way they thought they should be answered. Let's look at another type of prayer. This type of prayer has to do with you and your personal recovery. This is not the time to pray for your partner to get his act together spiritually so that you don't have to experience this growth yourself.

Lets look at some examples of prayers that early in the morning, may be helpful for partners:

❏ Please God, keep me out of his head, briefcase, etc.
❏ Please God, let me focus on my feelings.
❏ Please God, help me not to look at every woman as a threat, especially female sex addicts.
❏ Please God, if I get out of control, help me to call on you and then make a phone call to a group member.
❏ God, today I give control over to you.

The first thing in the morning, take time out to pray. Prayer at this point, does not mean that you have to believe in God. It simply means to pray. When the old timers in Alcoholics Anonymous went to their meetings, they didn't say, "Well if you believe in God, pray." They said, "get on your knees and pray." If you don't believe in God, imagine a conversation with a grandparent or other relative you love and respect. Say, "God, I don't believe in You, but I'm supposed to pray. I want to be a partner in recovery today. Would you help me stay sober today?" From that point on, you can discuss any of your issues that you want to talk to God about. God is able to handle the hurt, anger, fear, anxiety, and any other feelings you have kept from God.

Prayer is a way for you to change yourself behaviorally. The thoughts about your addict and his addiction can start early in the day. Prayer is preventative. This habit of going to God early in the day can put you in a spiritual place for yourself and give you added strength to get you through whatever your day may bring.

EMPOWERMENT EXERCISE #3

READING RECOVERY MATERIAL

Reading recovery material that is specifically related to sexual addiction and partner issues is important. There are currently only a few books on the market addressing partners specifically but plenty on co-dependency that you can read. It is very important to read some recovery material every day.

Reading is best when done in the morning. Partners of addicts need to be reminded of what may be in store for them today. Sometimes the recovery thoughts that you read about are the very tool that can get you out of a tough situation. The reading can give you the strength to fight for your recovery that day. It is important that you involve your mind in your recovery.

A list of reading materials is provided in the index. By now you can probably get a feeling that your morning is going to change. This can take five to fifteen minutes, and it will make a dramatic change in your day. You are worth getting the recovery you need so that you can restore yourself. You are going to learn a lot, not only about yourself, but about recovery in general so that you can get a picture of hope to integrate into your everyday life-style.

EMPOWERMENT EXERCISE #4

CALL SOMEONE

Calling someone in your recovery group can be liberating, as well as, a helpful tool in your recovery. Many of the partners I have had the privilege of working with report a time in their relationship with the sex addict that they felt alone, isolated from others. These partners have not been able to talk to anyone about "this"; no friends or family knew the secrets they kept to themselves. Some of these partners have moved away from their family and friends by the relationship with the sex addict or, because of the addict's behavior, they were isolated from family and friends.

Isolation definitely can get a partner into an emotionally unhealthy state. We often need others to "run things by" to see if our reality is in check. There may be times when red flags in your relationship with the sex addict might not have been ignored if you only had someone to talk to.

In recovery, you will need a real person to talk to. The ideal relationship is another recovering woman who is a member of COSA or S-Anon. In the real world, many reading this book will not have these groups in your local area. In this situation, you can :

- ❑ attend ALANON meetings (partners of alcoholics)- many of these alcoholics are sex addicts as well
- ❑ attend CODA groups (these are for co-dependency)
- ❑ start a support group yourself by contacting COSA or S-ANON (see back of the book for contact numbers)
- ❑ have a close friend walk through this process with you, someone without an agenda for you or your marriage
- ❑ Start with an objective therapist who thoroughly understands sex addiction and their partner's issues
- ❑ Join an online support group listed on our website at **www.sexaddict.com**

When you decide how your going to start and with whom, start as soon as possible. Phone calls are an ESSENTIAL part of early recovery. If you are using the support of a group member or friend, I strongly suggest you call daily to check in for the first 90 days. Together we get well, alone we stay unhealthy.

EMPOWERMENT EXERCISE #5

GOING TO MEETINGS

There are many women who have been in your situation. This is freeing to know, in that, you are not alone and you don't have to be. There are 12 Step support groups for partners of sex addicts. The people in these support groups can be a great help to you. You can find these groups by calling the national phone number listed in the back of this book and asking for a location in your area. You can also call information if you live in a metropolitan area and ask for *Co-Sex Addicts Anonymous (COSA)* or *S-Anon.* You can also find support groups by going to our links page at **www.sexaddict.com** or consider an on-line support group to help you if no group is available in your area. If you don't find one in your area you may have to start one yourself. It won't take long for others to join.

If you are fortunate enough to have a meeting in your area, attend! You may feel uncomfortable the first few minutes but after that, you will feel the warmth and support of women who can honestly nod their head when you say, "You know what I mean?"

They may not share the exact same problem as you, but they live with a lot of the same characteristics. You can learn what has worked for them, gain support for the decision you need to make in your relationship, and most of all you won't have to be "alone" any more.

The day I started to attend a group: _____

I attended _____ times a week.

EMPOWERMENT EXERCISE #6

EVENING PRAYER

Praying again in the evening may sound inconvenient for you, and it may be. You can read *Exercise #3, Early Prayer* again to be reminded that this is not something you have to like or agree with to do. Prayer is something that is best behaviorally to do daily. At the end of the day, if you have maintained your sanity, thank God.

Recovery isn't something you do by yourself, it is something you do with the help of God and others. If there are any other issues from the day you want to talk to God about, you can also bring them up at this time. It is important to end your day in a spiritual place in addition to starting the day in a spiritual place. The recovery program that is going to work is spiritual in nature. So, it is important to reestablish your own spirituality since you were born spirit, soul, and body. Make this a time of being thankful that you had a day of recovery.

The worst day in recovery with the support and information you have today, is something to be thankful for. Remember, even one generation ago they didn't know about sex addiction and there wasn't help for partners of sex addicts. So be thankful, and end your day in a conversation with the One who gave you a day of recovery.

EMPOWERMENT EXERCISE #7

THE FIVE COMMANDMENTS
A Ninety Day Check List

Recovery from being a sex addict's partner has some basic principles that when applied, help you sustain a recovery program. Early recovery is not simply understanding the facts nor is early recovery simply talking about sexual addiction issues. Recovery goes much deeper than talking about what was done in the past, rather it is moving into changing behaviors and life-styles.

The Five Commandments are simple and can be used much like a check list that you can put up on your wall or mirror at home. Write the commandments down and check off if you have done them today, this week, this month, and the first 90 days. This behavioral check list can assure you that you are putting behavior toward recovery as opposed to just coming to an understanding about it. Coming to an understanding is not the only answer. You may have been in pain for years and years and possibly have had behaviors that have been repeated many times. The Five Commandments, when put in place, give you an action plan to arrest the behaviors that you have been struggling with for so long while surviving with the sexual addiction affecting your partner.

Simply put, the Five Commandments are the last five behaviors you have read in Exercises #3-#7. These Five Commandments are simple:

1. <u>Pray</u> in the morning
2. <u>Read</u> recovery literature daily
3. <u>Call</u> someone in recovery daily
4. <u>Meetings</u> - attend Twelve-Step Meetings
5. <u>Pray</u> again, and thank God daily for recovery

The following check list on the next page will help you monitor your behaviors toward recovery.

DATE	PRAY	READ	CALL	MEET	PRAY		DATE	PRAY	READ	CALL	MEET	PRAY
1							48					
2							49					
3							50					
5							51					
7							52					
9							53					
11							54					
12							55					
13							56					
14							57					
15							58					
16							59					
17							60					
18							61					
19							62					
20							63					
21							64					
22							65					
23							66					
24							67					
25							68					
26							69					
27							70					
28							71					
29							72					
30							73					
31							74					
32							75					
33							76					
34							77					
35							78					
36							79					
37							80					
38							81					
39							82					
40							83					
41							84					
42							85					
43							86					
44							87					
45							88					
46							89					
47							90					

EMPOWERMENT EXERCISE #8

MAXIMIZED THINKING

The maximized thinking technique is easy to understand. Simply ask yourself daily, (especially during the first year of recovery), "Is this the most I can put into my recovery today?" If the answer is more "yes" than "no", you will find yourself progressing through recovery quite well. Maximized thinking plays a big part in early recovery.

Those who consistently do the Five Commandments (which you learned about in the previous exercise) as much as possible, will make tremendous gains with maximized thinking added to their personal, spiritual and sexual life-style. I have seen many partners of sex addicts who have chosen maximized thinking in their recovery who have experienced a much better social, spiritual, and sexual life-style.

One way I determine a partner's level of seriousness in early recovery, is by recovery behaviors. Intention, no matter how good, misleads you to think that you are in recovery when you actually are not. Remember not to base your recovery on the sex addict you may live with. The addicts recovery and motivation is their issue, and your recovery is your focus at this time.

The Five Commandments are a good check list to determine if you are applying maximized thinking or some other approach to what may be the hardest task of your life, that being recovery from life with a sex addict. If you are still reading up to this point, that is a good sign, but keep on going! Trust me when I say "you are worth your recovery," but nobody deserves recovery without effort, and nobody that I know gets recovery that way either. So, maximize the early part of your recovery, and you will have the rest of your life to thank yourself for the time you put in the beginning of your recovery.

19

EMPOWERMENT EXERCISE #9

BELIEVE BEHAVIOR

Throughout your relationship with your sexually addicted partner, you may have been promised that he would stop his addictive behavior. In recovery, I have found it most helpful only to believe a recovering addict's behavior. Addicts of any type have the ability to muster a form of emotional sincerity in a crisis that makes you want to believe them but shortly thereafter, he simply does not follow through with the behaviors he promised.

Only behaviors will tell you where your addict is in his recovery. The best thing about behaviors is that they are measurable. The surest way for an addict to recover from his addictive behavior is to complete the Five Commandments as much as possible the first 90 days. If you don't see these recovery behaviors, your probably looking at someone trying to recover by himself. The "self" program has never worked in the past, and for you to believe differently would put both of you in denial of the disease of sexual addiction. This mutual denial will probably lead to a relapse down the road.

Don't believe what your partner says, believe what he does. If you don't see it, don't make it up that it is happening. Staying in reality is what makes your recovery work.

EMPOWERMENT
EXERCISE #10

VERBAL REALITY

Addicts of any kind live in what I call "verbal reality." This means if they say it, it is true and if they say it passionately it is really true. The behavior and follow-through in weeks to come is not required for it to be true.

You must understand the sex addict's verbal reality; this is often how you are manipulated by the addict. The sex addict believes what he is saying while he is saying it, and to him, that is enough not to follow through with the behavior. That is why we discussed believing behavior.

Your only savior in the verbal reality is measurable behavior. He says "I love you" but acts out. The behavior is always the truth. He says he wants to change, but attends no meetings, makes no calls, the behavior is the truth. Don't be fooled by verbal reality and don't blame him if you buy what he says to you. In the past, your own desire to believe the best and not make measurable behaviors the issue set up a system you both were familiar with. The system is: he does what he wants. Says: "I love you" or "I'll change." You believe him, nothing changes and then you get to repeat this cycle again.

The way to stop this is to ask what behaviors he is committed to and where he is going to check off if he did them or not. Addicts themselves buy their verbal reality so YOU can't if you are going to recover.

EMPOWERMENT EXERCISE #11

_____

AM I A SEX ADDICT?

This question pops up many times by partners of sex addicts. They want to know if they did certain behaviors with their sexually addicted partner, are they a sex addict?

The long answer to this question would be answered in the *Final Freedom* which is available in an audio tape series or book. The simplest answer that I can give you here is as follows. A sex addict has sex to fix something inside whether it be neurological, psychological or both. Most partners have the frequency or types of sex with their partner to "keep him." These are two totally different reasons for having sex and therefore the majority of partners are not sex addicts.

To those that believe that they still are addicted to sex and have a history of sexual acting out behaviors that precedes this current relationship, I would recommend the book *She Has A Secret*; *Understanding Female Sexual Addiction* along with the workbook *Secret Solutions*. If you need further help to decide if you are a sex addict, you may also need to see a therapist specializing in sexual addiction.

EMPOWERMENT
EXERCISE #12

WHAT SHOULD I KNOW?

You have probably suffered in many ways from your partner's addiction possibly including his inability to be emotionally intimate, financial loss, humiliation, the list goes on. If you are deciding to work this out with him as he recovers, he is fortunate and in my experience he would be in the minority in their Twelve Step group.

"What should I tell her?" is one of the first questions I hear from an addict who wants to protect his marriage. The answer is situational. I will offer the possible options and you may need a therapist also to help you in this area.

OPTIONS

1. Have him tell you everything. (These details will never be forgotten)
2. Have him tell you types of behaviors he struggles with.
3. Have him tell you vaguely without details "I had an affair."
4. Have him never tell you.

Another issue after you decide what he should tell you is, how much do you want to be included in his recovery process? In most cases, you will not understand his fantasy, masturbation, pornography or other behavioral struggles. You are not his sponsor. His sponsor needs to be someone of the same sex. It is helpful for you to be aware of where your partner is in his recovery so you may want to agree on some questions you can ask that will be answered honestly.

Examples of the types of questions that you may want to ask about his recovery are:

1. Have you crossed your bottom line?
2. Have you masturbated?
3. How often are you going to meetings?
4. Review the five commandments: Prayer, reading, call, meetings, prayer
5. Have you acted out with another person?

In my experience with other sex addicts, it is better to plan a weekly or biweekly meeting with your partner to discuss these questions. This can prevent you from coming up with questions at any-time or during an argument. If you are staying with him during his recovery, it is appropriate and can be therapeutic for you both to keep it in a manageable session. If you have specific questions about these issues, you may want to speak to a therapist.

23

EMPOWERMENT EXERCISE #13

STOP LOOKING

As a partner of a sex addict, you may have picked up some unusual behaviors in order to survive in your relationship. Some partners of sex addicts acquire a behavior of "looking." They look to see if they can find attractive women before their partner sees them. Then the questions begin. "Did he see her?" "What is he thinking about?" "How can I look like that?" "Did he look back at her?" Some partners had this behavior even before knowing their partner was a sex addict. Some did it after they found out.

Every attractive woman is not the enemy or a threat to your relationship. Sex addiction is the enemy. To help yourself stop looking, comparing, and questioning, I have listed some tips I have shared with sex addicts who need to quit looking in other ways.

1.   The 3 Second Rule - if you notice you are looking at your partner to see if he is looking at someone else, count to three then look away.
2.   Wear a rubber band on your wrist for 30 days. When you "look", snap it. This will help slow down all the anxiety.
3.   Call someone in your recovery group and talk about it.
4.   Pray for the woman you are looking at. She may need some extra prayer.

EMPOWERMENT
EXERCISE #14

BLAME GAME

The sex addict in your life has most likely caused some negative situations in your life. These negatives have no doubt greatly affected you, especially if it has happened over many years. The sex addict is probably responsible for many things such as neglect and abuse. He is also responsible for his addiction and his recovery from this addiction.

The damage he has done to you is his responsibility. When he does his 9th Step in recovery, (about a year or more in recovery) he will be sober enough to own this behavior and actually feel the pain for it. Don't expect this immediately. He will probably be emotionally and spiritually unable to do this any earlier.

What you do with this damage is your responsibility. You may have little to do with getting hit by a car, but you have everything to do with your healing from being hit. Blaming him and staying there too long can keep you and the relationship unhealthy. Assess the damage you have incurred and become active in your personal recovery from the damage.

What you become in your recovery is totally and only up to you. You live in a culture that allows you choices in every direction of your life. Move your thinking into solutions instead of problems and you will accelerate your progress in recovery. You deserve the best quality of life by taking care of your needs and taking responsibility for yourself. The quicker you move away from a state of blame to a state of activity toward recovery, the quicker you get through this process.

EMPOWERMENT EXERCISE #15

MY WORST FEAR

Living with the realization that your partner is a sex addict can bring a whole new set of questions, feelings, and fears about many things such as: "Did he act out with prostitutes? Men? Someone I know? Does he have AIDS? Do I have AIDS? Has he committed illegal acts?" These and more are some of the fears partners of sex addicts endure.

You are definitely rational to have these and other questions. The key is how to handle them so you don't get unhealthy. Some with active imaginations have painted pictures in their minds about what he "probably" did in his acting out.

Fears often lose their overwhelming power when they are identified and communicated to someone else. On a piece of paper, make a list of your worst fears. Take this list and share it with your recovery friend or group. Sharing these fears can help you process them and get them out of your head. If you still have concerns after this exercise it may be helpful to make a telephone appointment with Dr. Weiss (See Appendix).

EMPOWERMENT EXERCISE #16

ME, ACTING OUT?

Many partners early in recovery don't believe they have problems themselves. It is their partner who has all the problems they think. Granted, his addiction is usually more devastating and definitely the priority early on for the couple's survival. It takes a while but usually when the addict stabilizes in his recovery, it is about time to look at yourself.

An addiction in its simplest form is using something or someone to medicate feelings. Another definition is "If the behavior doesn't make sense and they keep doing it, it is probably an addiction." Both definitions have fit many partners of sex addicts or as they call themselves in 12 Step recovery groups "co-sex addicts."

How does a co-sex addict "act out"? There are many different ways this can actually happen. Here are only a few:

1. Spiritualizing the problem
2. Checking up on him
3. Scoping out women he might be looking at
4. Looking for more proof
5. Not being able to separate when it makes sense
6. Spiritualizing or rationalizing staying together when he is not recovering
7. Feeling threatened or insecure around other women when with your partner
8. Trying to think about what he "might be" thinking about
9. Being controlling
10. Not having sex or being hyper-sexual
11. Pretending you're in a perfect relationship
12. Changing your boundaries with your partner
13. Shaming him
14. Rages
15. Sarcasm
16. Hitting him
17. Fantasizing about him acting out
18. Using his problem not to deal with your feelings
19. Reinforcing your fears of abandonment
20. Other _____
21. Other _____
22. Other _____

If any of these are your acting out behaviors, you can circle them for future reference. If you have others, feel free to write them in. Share these with your recovery friend or group.

EMPOWERMENT EXERCISE #17

STAYING SOBER

Once you identify what your acting out behavior is, you can make an action plan for your recovery from these behaviors. First list your top five acting out behaviors.

1. _____
2. _____
3. _____
4. _____
5. _____

Write the person's name you will be accountable to for these behaviors.

_____

What are alternative behaviors or preventative behaviors you need to make to stay sober from these behaviors?

1. _____
2. _____
3. _____
4. _____
5. _____

What are your consequences if you don't follow through with your recovery plan?

1. _____
2. _____
3. _____
4. _____
5. _____

What is your start date to implement your recovery plan?

_____

EMPOWERMENT
EXERCISE #18

FEELING ALONE

Alone is a feeling. It is often a feeling that many partners of sex addicts are familiar with, but rarely are they comfortable with feeling. This exercise is designed to allow the feeling "alone" not to be so overwhelming or scary.

     Exercise: On a piece of paper, write out three experiences of being alone that you are currently having.

     Example: I feel alone when my husband walks far in front of me in public places.

After you have written these experiences, write three more experiences of feeling alone when you were a child, teenager, or young adult. In writing these feelings out, are there any correlations between your past aloneness and your present alone issues? For some, the feeling or fear of being alone is a family of origin issue that may need to be looked into further at sometime in your recovery. One of the ways of dealing with fear is to practice it.

     Exercise: Feel the alone feeling and hold the feeling for 15-30 seconds. Some people put their body in a position that also reflects "alone," similar to a mime. Do this twice daily for a week. During the second week, double your time to 30-60 seconds, twice daily. In a couple weeks, you will have practiced the alone feeling enough that you will know how to master this feeling and not be its slave. Practice this as often as needed. Be okay with feeling alone. Alone doesn't have to be a big feeling. It can be like other feelings you have that don't paralyze but allow you to go on with your life.

EMPOWERMENT
EXERCISE #19

ABANDONMENT

I would like to share with you an experience, I was fortunate to have, in a national COSA conference I went to several years ago. I was sharing with 40 COSA members of various socio-economic statuses from all over the country. I asked the group one question. What do you fear the most? The entire group of 40 people said one word in unison: "Abandonment."

Abandonment issues run very deep in many partners of sex addicts. It is important to address this early in your recovery. Abandonment is a type of fear and often our worst fear. We know intellectually fear is rarely reality but if you believe or have faith in your fear, all the results from this belief will be very real. This fear often paralyzes partners so they won't grow or change or face something in reality.

In the below space, write out your fears in general and your fears of being abandoned by your partner. Review this list with your recovery friend or group members and then make a list of options for each fear.

EXAMPLE: Fear   Plan

1.   Fear of not being able to support self   Learn computer skills by next year and
      and children   separate if I need to at that time

2.   _____   _____

3.   _____   _____

4.   _____   _____

5.   _____   _____

6.   _____   _____

7.   _____   _____

8.   _____   _____

9.   _____   _____

10.   _____   _____

EMPOWERMENT EXERCISE #20

ALONE: FACT

There is a sad fact that many partners of sex addicts realize at some point in their recovery. The fact is that they have been alone in their relationship. The lack of support, nurturing, intimacy, and for some even sexually, can become a painful fact to process in your recovery.

Does he love you? Probably as much as an addict can love anyone in his disease. I have heard many partners say, "I feel like an object or an employee of his, not his wife." The fact of being alone is important to acknowledge for your recovery. In the spaces below, check off those areas you are alone in your relationship to a sex addict.

❑Spiritually

❑Socially (no couple friends)

❑Financially (he handles it all)

❑Sexually (his terms only)

❑Parenting

❑Supporting you

❑Listening/hearing you

❑Being cherished

❑Dating

EMPOWERMENT EXERCISE #21

HOT BUTTON

The *hot button* is the only way I can describe what happens to some partners of sex addicts when they are around female sex addicts. Female sex addicts send out strong sexual energy whether passively or blatantly. Female sex addicts may be predatory in nature much like some male sex addicts.

I have spent countless hours in sessions covering stories where women went public places with their recovering sex addict and boom, the hot button was pushed. A female sex addict shows up and you feel uncomfortable, threatened, less than, and often times angry. Remember, this is your button that is going off. It doesn't mean that your addict partner isn't taking care of himself in this situation.

Sometimes you may take all these feelings out on your partner, and he may truly not be in trouble in his recovery around this particular person in this setting at this time. Don't make this about him. This is about you. The way you may need to take care of yourself in this situation is to get on the phone ("Excuse me, I forgot to make a call to someone.") with your recovery friend or group. Own your own feelings and process this with the person on the phone, not the sex addict.

EMPOWERMENT EXERCISE #22

THE VICTIM
An Emotional State of Mind

Playing "the victim" is a major strategy of the sex addict. It appears that no matter what the situation is, he plays the victim where he has been hurt more than you. Playing "the victim" is tricky to catch, but once you identify this behavior, it will usually lead to something the addict doesn't want to take responsibility for. The victim is in an emotional state, and you can not reason with this behavior. The victim will somehow make you believe that your behavior was worse than his.

Remember the victim is an emotional state. Don't reason with this behavior. The victim also gets other people to rally around him. This is another way of manipulating others to do what he should be doing. As long as you submit to this victim behavior, it will continue to operate.

To address this issue with your partner, I suggest you pick a public place like a restaurant. Select a time when you think he is sober headed, then state that you notice a dynamic with him you would like to share. Discuss "the victim" and state what your boundaries are going to be. Then be consistent with these boundaries. He may or may not respond with some anger when you begin to initiate change in this area.

"The victim" has protected the addict from so many hard realities about himself that to grow beyond this is painful and requires a lot of honesty on his part. Be patient but persistent with the victim and one more time, don't reason with the victim, you are wasting your time. Simply acknowledge that it "sounds like the victim" or "the victims out we will talk about this later." If these conversations get heated, call your recovery friend or group members for support.

EMPOWERMENT
EXERCISE #23

PAIN AND ME

As a partner of a sex addict, there is no doubt that you have experienced pain to one degree or another. Some have experienced a variety of pain from being in a relationship with a sex addict or other type of addict. Other painful experiences in your past could have been sexual, physical, or emotional neglect or abuse.

Pain demands medication. For partners of sex addicts, there are several different options to medicate pain. Check off the ones that apply to you and share these with your recovery friend or group. If you need professional help with these issues, please give this gift to yourself because if you can heal the pain, you wont need the medicine.

- ❑ Not eating
- ❑ Overeating
- ❑ Anger/Rage
- ❑ Sarcasm
- ❑ Spending/Debting
- ❑ Controlling
- ❑ No Sex/Hypersexual
- ❑ Unhealthy Relationships
- ❑ Obsessive Cleaning
- ❑ Alcohol/Drugs
- ❑ Hyper-religious
- ❑ Obsessive Exercise
- ❑ Living For The Children
- ❑ Obsessing About The Addict
- ❑ Depression
- ❑ Other _____
- ❑ Other _____
- ❑ Other _____

EMPOWERMENT EXERCISE #24

THE CON

Many partners have communicated to me that they have felt "conned." This partner is not who they thought he was and this is definitely not what they signed up for. This feeling is legitimate, and most partners have been conned by the sex addict. Let's face it. If he were to say, "I'm a sex addict," you wouldn't have given him the time of day.

The normal sex addict con goes like this: You meet. He thinks your the world's best lover, friend, and you are beautiful. This can go on for weeks or months. Once he knows your self esteem has shifted to depend on his praise, he has you. This shift can happen before or after marriage. After the shift occurs, you can't do anything right-especially sex, and your not so smart either. He continues to actively chisel away at your self-esteem. This, combined with isolation from friends and family, leaves you to a large degree dependent on him. If he can make you financially dependent as well, that is even better for him. Then you can't leave him.

This pattern is familiar to many sex addiction relationships. If you have experienced this, your pain is probably great. He did all this to you so he could stay in control and act out. You can be rightfully angry. If you feel you have been conned, write out a letter or a list of how you have been conned by your addict and share it with a recovery person or group.

EMPOWERMENT EXERCISE #25

PAST FAILURES

Some partners have clued into their partner's early on that something was wrong but they didn't know what. Others knew he had his collection of movies or materials. In many cases, you as a partner may have tried to control the sex addict's behavior. You may have been more sexual, less sexual, used anger or shame to try to get this problem to stop.

Whatever the approaches you have used in the past, I would like you to list these:

_____ 1. _____

_____ 2. _____

_____ 3. _____

_____ 4. _____

_____ 5. _____

In the line next to your approach write a yes or no if you feel this technique was successful. In many cases the above may not have been successful. Review this with your recovery friend. You may want to periodically use this as a reference before you try another approach or before you try something you already know doesn't work.

EMPOWERMENT EXERCISE #26

THE BRIBE

The bribe is a dynamic I see when working with partners of sex addicts. The concept is simple: you and the partner agree to put up the appearance that everything is normal in exchange for you taking care of the children or remaining unemployed.

You can tell the bribe is in a relationship when the husband's first line of defense is the checkbook. He believes he is paying you off, so what are you complaining about? If you don't like it, he will find someone who will.

There are several dynamics here. He knows your abandonment issues. He tried to beat your self-esteem so low that you don't believe you could ever take care of yourself. He sees you as an object in his life providing a function. For the bribe dynamic to work, there has to be a volunteer to take the bribe. Some do this exchange willingly especially if they live financially well, others do it reluctantly because they feel trapped.

Breaking the bribe pattern is a process. 1) You must first accept that it is true and be honest about your participating in this; (remember only volunteers not victims) 2) Make a short-or-long term structured goal to stop taking the bribe. A short-term example may be to get a job. Long-term would be to let him pay for your education and then become independent.

Breaking the bribe dynamic doesn't mean you have to leave. You can become independent within a relationship, and you have to be independent before you can be interdependent in a relationship.

If you're taking the bribe, be honest. Write out exactly the bribe your taking (house, car or other) and what you know you expected to provide in the relationship and socially outside the relationship. After writing this out, discuss your bribe and your goals for growth with your recovery friend.

EMPOWERMENT EXERCISE #27

MY CHOICES

Being in a relationship with a sex addict does bring up the question of do I stay or leave? These questions are legitimate. In this exercise, I want to expose you to some options you may or may not have thought of before.

1. Stay and stay sick - This option is taken by those who do not desire change or growth Familiar, no matter how bad, is better than different, no matter how good. Those who take this option rarely consider what is familiar today will be a walk in the park compared to his continuing disease.

2. Stay and be uninvolved - It is his problem; he needs to recover; and, I don't want or need to know anything.

3. Stay and be overinvolved - Tell him what to read, what therapist to see, what groups to go to and you're putting more energy into his recovery than he is.

4. Stay and both recover - Both work their own recovery program. Both have support people, both work the steps, and, if therapy is needed for the marriage or either or both, they get it as soon as possible. This option has the highest success rate of couples staying married and having real intimacy.

5. Stay conditionally - State the boundaries or conditions you will stay in during the relationship. If these boundaries are violated or conditions not met, separate from each other until these conditions are met.

6. Divorce - Get a lawyer and leave.

The above are real choices that many women have already had to make. This choice is yours to make. This choice affects the rest of you and your family's life. Give yourself time to think through this, and, if you need professional help with this, I have seen many women through the choices they made. Discuss the choice from the above (or your own) options with your recovery group or friend.

EMPOWERMENT EXERCISE #28

HOW TO LEAVE

It is very important you consider how you are going to leave this relationship if that is what you intend to do. This can not be an emotional decision, if it is, you will usually abandon your needs and possibly your children's needs also.

Before you leave, write out your plans of how you are going to take care of yourself or your family. Some women make anywhere from one month-to-two-year plans to leave. I've seen such behaviors as: buying new clothes so when they leave, they have clothes to last for a few years; buying months worth of groceries slowly so the family is taken care of while the transition occurs; going to classes to increase professional skills; and many others, most involving the saving of money.

Before you leave, know what your goals are in leaving. To separate, to hopefully reconcile a marriage, to use separation to see if you really can make it with alimony, child support and work, or to divorce. If you need legal information, get what you need so that any decision you are making is the most informed decision.

Write your goals and your plans out on a piece of paper, share these with your recovery friend or group members.

EMPOWERMENT EXERCISE #29

LAWYERS

Talking to lawyers can be a costly experience if your not prepared. It is best to talk to lawyers calmly with your questions already written out with space to write down your answers so you are not paying for the attorney's time. The only time you don't pay for a lawyer's time is the first consult meeting (and make sure it is free before you make the appointment). I recommend you see at least five attorneys for free asking the same questions as before until you feel informed, and before you decide on anyone to represent you.

In your questions, ask about fees. What is the paralegal rate? The lawyers rate? Ask who does what in a case like yours. Does he/she charge for phone calls. What is the estimated cost of your case and why? The answers to these questions should also be stated in the contract from your lawyer.

EMPOWERMENT EXERCISE #30

BE FAIR

His recovery is his recovery and your recovery will be yours and the couple recovery will be a shared responsibility. The sex addict is what we call the identified patient. He is the one with the problem. His problem would, in most cases, cause enough damage through neglect that any primary relationship would be affected.

Many partners have made demands on their addict's recovery without any awareness that they themselves are doing little about their own recovery. A friend of mine who is married to an alcoholic wanted me to join her in nagging her husband to go to AA. I asked her if she was going to ALANON. She said no. I said, "If your not willing to make changes, why are you asking your husband to?" Needless to say, we never had another conversation about her husband going to AA.

What I am saying here is to be fair. If you are not willing to go to recovery meetings or make calls, you may want to think about this as it relates to your recovery. He will need to do the behaviors of recovery and the partners that do better are those who have recovery behaviors themselves. So in recovery, be fair to your partner and be fair to yourself.

EMPOWERMENT
EXERCISE #31

FIRST EXPERIENCE

The first time you have sex can be a highly formative experience. For some the first sexual experience shaped what their belief about sex; what they believe their role is in sex; what they believe or expect their role is in sex; how connected they need to be during sex; how emotionally intimate they need to be to have sex; who sex is for, and is sex fun?

This first incident for many was clumsy at best and traumatic at worst. For some partners, it is very helpful on a separate sheet of paper to answer these questions as to what you learned in your first sexual experience.

1.	What do you believe about sex from this experience?
2.	What is your role in sex from this experience?
3.	What do you believe the man's role in sex is?
4.	How connected were you in this experience?
5.	How emotionally intimate were you in this experience?
6.	Who is sex for from this experience?
7.	Is sex fun from this experience?

After you answer these questions, go back through and answer them as they relate to your current sexual relationship. Share with your recovery friend or group any insight you have learned in this process. Make a note of that on a piece of paper.

EMPOWERMENT EXERCISE #32

INTUITION HISTORY

Your intuition is very much a part of who you are. It is the sense within that tells if things are okay or not. Intuition is not an intellectual process. Your intuition has probably tried to speak to you many times. For some partners, they have almost stopped feeling their intuition because they have denied it so many times. My experience with intuition is that when you honor it, it is correct almost 90% or more of the time.

When the final realization does hit that your partner is a sex addict, you may remember questioning things that didn't seem totally right. Go back through your relationship with this sex addict and see if there are places where your intuition was trying to talk to you.

On a piece of paper, make a list of these times and if they line up with anything you presently know about his addiction. Share this list with your recovery friend or group members. Often this exercise affirms to the partner that she was right about her intuition in the past even without the facts. It is important for you to realize your intuition is an important and valid part of who you are. Your intuition will be restored further as you honor it and go through the process of recovery.

EMPOWERMENT EXERCISE #33

STEP ONE

"We admitted that we were powerless over our co-dependency with the sex addict and that our lives had become unmanageable."

The Twelve Steps of recovery began with Alcoholics Anonymous in 1933. These steps have helped millions of people recover from alcoholism and have been adapted to help others from many other addictions. In the appendix you will find the Twelve Steps adapted for "Codependents of Sex Addicts." Steps One through Twelve are placed throughout this book in a specific order to which I believe you will be at the best place to work that particular step at that particular time. This is why it is important to follow the order of the exercises in this book.

Step One is the most important step of all. In Step One, you place your feet on the path to recovery. "We" means that you will have others involved with you in your recovery. Recovery is a team participation sport. "We admitted" is not all of Step One. Some people attend meetings and never do a full Step One. They just admit that they are a partner of a sex addict much like the alcoholic who admits he is an alcoholic while taking a drink.

Step One has us admit that we are "powerless." Powerlessness is different than being addicted. Being addicted to cocaine could mean that if you saw some cocaine, "you couldn't help yourself" and you would use the cocaine. Powerlessness means that if you saw some cocaine, you would run out of there, call someone, and try any new behaviors to avoid what once controlled your life.

Many lives are tainted with the unmanageability that sex addiction brought to your life through your addict. In your recovery, sanity and order will replace the "crazies" and the chaos. Step One is the beginning to a life-style of recovery. In the workbook, Beyond Love, I provide over 20 pages that allow you to explore and experience Step One. This is how important I feel it is.

Behaviors that support Step One are:

BEHAVIOR		YES	NO
1.	Praying	_____	_____
2.	Reading	_____	_____
3.	Phone calls	_____	_____
4.	Meetings	_____	_____
5.	Staying accountable	_____	_____
6.	Creativity comes to your recovery	_____	_____

EMPOWERMENT EXERCISE #34

MY STORY

It is helpful in recovery to write out your story. Your story is unique to anyone else and will give you insight about yourself.

On another sheet of paper, write out your story with these general guidelines. The first section should be "Where I have come from." Here, discuss family of origin issues, neglects, abandonment abuses. The second section is "My relationship history." Highlight types of people you dated, had sexual relationships with from beginning to the current relationships and any patterns you see in this aspect of your life. The next section is "How I arrived at recovery." This section includes the major or minor events that made you choose a recovery process for yourself as a partner of a sex addict. The next section is "Where I am today with my life." The last section is "Where I hope to be in the future." When you are finished with your story, share it with your recovery friend or group members.

EMPOWERMENT
EXERCISE #35

MY SPONSOR

A sponsor in a 12 step group is similar to a mentor. She is someone who has been where you are and knows how to get further in recovery than you. She is someone you will call regularly and talk to about recovery. She will be someone who will encourage you to do your step work and she will hold you accountable to goals you have set for yourself in recovery.

In picking a sponsor, you probably want to listen to others in your support group who are really in recovery. This would probably be someone who isn't reporting her latest "crazy" story but rather is working her steps and it is best if she has finished her fifth step before you may want her to be your sponsor. This eliminates her helping you in the midst her own garbage. After the fifth step, there is a lot less shame and someone can be much healthier to help you.

Utilizing a sponsor relationship can help tremendously in not feeling alone in your recovery. This relationship hopefully will allow you to see that there is more in recovery for you in the future. To pick a sponsor, ask someone when they think would be a good time to talk about this; and, if you mutually agree, this would be your sponsor.

EMPOWERMENT EXERCISE #36

IDENTIFYING & COMMUNICATING FEELINGS

Any partner may have difficulty with identifying feelings. If you have a feeling, you can usually fix it by staying busy or obsessing about your addict.

Most partner's of sex addicts have not received any training in the area of feelings from their family of origin. Feelings are a skill that you can develop and acquire levels of mastery once you are trained. This is similar to growing up and not learning how to maintain a car. It doesn't mean that you are less intelligent or worthwhile because you can't fix a car. You would be simply untrained. If you were to take a class on car maintenance, you would probably be a good mechanic. The difference is that the skills you may have been exposed to and learned make you more skilled.

Expressing feelings, in your recovery, is very important for several reasons. Some are mentioned below.

1. In the past, if you had a feeling, you probably would not know what it was. But if you ignored it by keeping busy, the feeling would go away. In this process, you may not have learned to identify feelings and hence could not meet your own real needs.

2. As a relapse prevention of old behaviors, if you can identify your feelings, you may better know how to handle or manage these feelings so as to prevent relapses.

3. If a cycle or relapses occur, you may be able to track down what emotion(s) preceded this and move forward in your recovery.

5. Mastering your feelings can allow more intimacy into your life. It will make your spiritual, social, and even your sex life better, too.

In the first month or so of your recovery, the feelings-identification exercise may be one of the harder exercises in this book. The discipline you put into this exercise will have lifelong benefits in every area of your life including relationships, parenting, work, recovery, spirituality, and your social life. It may also save you from financial mistakes because your intuition will become more active in your decision making process. (continued on next page)

47

The feelings exercise is simple. Fill in the blanks. An example is given below.

1.   I feel _(feeling word)_ when _____. (present tense)
2.   I first remember feeling _(same feeling word)_ when _____. (past tense)

EXAMPLE:

1.   I feel Calm when I am on the lake in a boat with a friend.
2.   I first remember feeling calm when I was 12 years old my sister and I identified shapes of animals from the clouds in the sky while lying on the grass.

The goal is to have experiences. In computer terms, you have an emotional data base, but this data base has no file names so you can't access the files nor can you utilize this data. This exercise, if you do two or more daily for a month to six weeks, will make your road in recovery a lot smoother. Those who do this in their recovery development early, never regret it later. Those who don't do this exercise, always regret it. So, I strongly encourage you to take the time to do this exercise today and for the next several weeks.

A list of feelings that you can utilize for your feelings exercises is located in the Appendix of this book. The list is in alphabetical order. You can pick out your feelings randomly in any manner you choose.

FEELINGS COMMUNICATION

When you have ten or more of your feelings identified, it is important that you begin to communicate them to a safe person. A safe person in your recovery group or a person who you are accountable to can be helpful at this. Their role is simply to listen, not really give feedback. If you choose your spouse, make sure this is safe for you and again, make sure your examples do not involve him in any way!!!

If you involve your partner, he can do the exercise and identify and communicate feelings back to you also. This can be a great opportunity to develop intimacy. If these experiences turn into disagreements, the exercise is being done wrong and you may need to pick another person or a therapist to do them with.

When sharing your feelings, it is important to maintain eye contact with the person you are sharing them with. This eye contact with a person may feel uncomfortable at first, but will eventually be comfortable to you. This is part of the benefit of this exercise. If you do this exercise with your spouse, it is imperative that no feedback be given to the spouse sharing a feeling.

EMPOWERMENT EXERCISE #37

DANGEROUS "E" ZONES
Your "Emotional" Zones

During your recovery, especially after completing your feeling exercises, you will become better acquainted with yourself and your feelings. Being aware of your feelings will be helpful, but it will not make them less difficult. In your recovery journey, you will find that some feelings are difficult for you to manage. Some of these feelings may include but are in no way limited to: fear, aloneness, abandonment, rejection, need or hopelessness.

These difficult feelings are what I call the dangerous "E" zones. They are feelings that you have skillfully avoided or medicated. They represent a cluster of feelings that you rarely allowed yourself to feel.

During your recovery, you need to find out what your dangerous "E" zones are. The easiest way is to take the feelings list and put a mark by those feelings you believe to be most difficult for you. List these feeling words below.

_____

_____

_____

EMPOWERMENT
EXERCISE # 38

ACTION PLANS FOR MY FEELINGS

In the previous exercise, you listed the feelings that could be your dangerous "E" zones. In this exercise, you will take the time to give yourself several options if you get into one of these zones. Having a written plan ahead of time helps a lot in recovery. This exercise will be a greater help if you can practice and hold the feeling for 15 seconds and then implement a plan of your choice. This practice will help when the real battle is on.

The following is an example to practice.

I feel bored.   Hold this bored feeling 15-30 seconds. Call someone in the program.

Below list the feelings that are dangerous "E" zones for you and list three behavioral options for that feeling. For example:

Bored

1. Call someone
2. Go to a meeting
3. Exercise

_____

1. _____
2. _____
3. _____

_____

1. _____
2. _____
3. _____

_____

1. _____
2. _____
3. _____

_____

1. _____
2. _____
3. _____

_____

1. _____
2. _____
3. _____

_____

1. _____
2. _____
3. _____

EMPOWERMENT EXERCISE #39

MY WORST MOMENT

A tool that can help you maintain recovery is having a negative experience locked in, almost memorized. This maximizes the pain and minimizes the pleasure of living the way you used to. For some, this picture could possibly be your partner getting picked up by the police, the day you received a phone call from "her," or the day you found his stash of porn. For others, their worst picture is contracting a sexually transmitted disease. These are only a few experiences. You may have one or more painful moments. You may want to write down these experiences to remind yourself.

After you write down these experiences, picture it in your mind as vividly as you can and feel the feelings. Practice this picture 2 to 3 times a day for three days. Rehearsing this image and feeling will make you ready to beat the desire to go back and live minimizing this addiction.

EMPOWERMENT EXERCISE #40

CALLING CARD

In recovery, as we discussed earlier, a phone call may be your only link to reality. In a moment, the pain or other feelings can sweep you off your feet and have you swirling in thoughts, pictures, devices and an entire host of feelings. It is as if you fall off a boat and it moves away leaving you in a storm. Somehow you need to connect to the boat so someone, anyone, can throw you a life preserver to save your life.

During the storm, you can pull out your phone card, call someone and be pulled safely back to the shore of recovery. If you were left to yourself, you may drown.

Simply put, keep phone numbers in your purse, car, home and your office so at any place and anytime you can call someone when you feel the storm coming. Remember you don't recover by yourself. It is much better to call first than to relapse into old behaviors and then have to call later. The calling card is one tool that can save you so make yours as soon as possible.

EMPOWERMENT EXERCISE #41

HAVING BOUNDARIES

While living with a sex addict, you will definitely need to learn how to have boundaries. Most sex addicts do not have very good boundaries when it comes to their primary partner. As with any type of addiction, this disease makes a person more selfish, manipulative, and at times hostile when confronted with a boundary. The partner of an addict needs to be fully committed to a boundary to be successful in introducing it to their addict.

A boundary is basically a line you draw "in the sand" which, if violated, has consequences to those who wish to violate them. There is a natural order to establishing boundaries.

1.   Identify the boundary
2.   Identify the consequence
3.   Enforce the consequence
4.   Give yourself a consequence if you don't enforce it
5.   Be accountable for your boundaries

In the next few pages, we will discuss boundaries as it relates to several areas of your life with a sex addict.

NOTE: Don't start discussing boundaries with your partner until you read this whole section on boundaries.

AREAS NEEDING BOUNDARIES

No two couples are alike. One couple has problems with boundaries in one area, while other couples have difficulties with boundaries in other areas. Below, check the areas in your current relationship where there are boundary problems.

❑communication
❑social behavior
❑dating
❑sex
❑money
❑anger

EMPOWERMENT EXERCISE #42

BEGINNING WITH BOUNDARIES

In the areas below, assign yourself a boundary you would like to see in your relationship with your partner.

Communication: (Example - To stay in the room when I am speaking) _____

_____

Social Behavior: (Example - Not to flirt with other women) _____

_____

Dating: (Example - To have a regular date night) _____

_____

Sex: (Example - Sex with our eyes open only) _____

_____

Money: (Example - No spending over _____ dollars without the other's consent)

_____

_____

Anger: (Example - No throwing things) _____

_____

EMPOWERMENT
EXERCISE #43

CONSEQUENCES

A boundary is not a boundary without the ability to enforce a consequence. Here you need to be extremely careful. Boundaries are not a way to complain, blame and not change. Consequences are for the result of changing behavior. In the below space, write enforceable consequences (not threats) to the previous boundaries you wrote.

Communication: (Example - When you leave the room while I am speaking, I will go for a one hour drive alone.)

_____

_____

Social Behavior: (Example - When you flirt, I will take a cab home immediately.)

_____

_____

Dating: (Example - No date, _____ task will not be completed by me this week.)

_____

_____

Sex: (Example - If you close your eyes, I stop)

_____

_____

Anger: (Example - If something is thrown, I call 911.)

_____

_____

EMPOWERMENT EXERCISE #44

ENFORCING CONSEQUENCES

Remember once a boundary is established, it will be tested. If a boundary is not enforced, it is just a threat and the addict will just go on his way since he has been threatened before. Enforcing a consequence is the hardest part of making and maintaining a boundary. Enforcing consequences on a consistent basis WILL change behavior.

If every time an addict throws something at you, he has to go to the police station or jail, after a few times, the throwing will stop. The consistent reinforcement of a boundary will relandscape your relationship.

If you respect yourself, they will respect you. If you need support in this process, use your support people in the process.

EMPOWERMENT
EXERCISE #45

YOUR CONSEQUENCES

    In many addictive relationships, the addict has chipped away at his partner's self-esteem and self-worth. You are worthy of having boundaries, but often you may not feel so under the addicts manipulative ploys to keep things the way they were (his way).

    Many partners need help around creating boundaries. In the section below, write out what **your** consequence will be if you don't follow through with your partner's consequence.

Communication: _____

_____

Social Behavior: _____

_____

Dating: _____

_____

Sex:_____

_____

Money: _____

_____

Anger: _____

_____

EMPOWERMENT EXERCISE #46

_____

ACCOUNTABILITY & SUPPORT

Establishing and maintaining boundaries around an addictive person is a hard and long process. The best situation during this time is to have one person, or a group of people, you can lean on for support when things get worse before they get better. Within this support person or group, an element of accountability also exists.

When you start a new boundary with the addict, let people in your support circle know what is going on, and solicit their availability if you need it. You can be there for others, and they can be there for you. Looking someone or a group in the face to report your progress is an important and often necessary element to be successful in having and maintaining boundaries.

You are worth having boundaries and as you do, your relationship will change and become healthier. Together with a support person or group you can make it through this process.

EMPOWERMENT EXERCISE #47

ONE AT A TIME

As we have already discussed, boundaries with your partner is a process. This is not a black or white situation. We must look at our relationship to see which boundaries need to be implemented now so that we can build our confidence in this beginning process.

The best way to start is with a boundary you have enough desire to see through until it is achieved. Start with only one boundary. The heat may go up momentarily. Be ready to be called "controlling" or see some other way the addict may display himself as a victim in this process.

Stick to your guns and your support group and you will see changes occur. When you feel like going to the next boundary, go through the same process and run it by your accountability group or person and begin again. Remember you are worth a relationship with boundaries. If you believe this and behave this way, you will probably have this happen one boundary at a time.

EMPOWERMENT
EXERCISE #48

MY VERY OWN SEXUAL BOUNDARIES

By now you are probably getting the sense that recovery from living with a sex addict has something to do with identifying and maintaining boundaries. This is true of any recovery, whether it is alcohol, drugs, sex or food. With sexual addiction recovery, you definitely need to address the sex act itself and identify what is healthy for you and your partner.

The history of your relationship with the sex addict may be long and scarred by his addiction. I have worked with couples where the addict involved his partner in sexual behaviors that they did not want to perform. These events were traumatic for you. If these situations have occurred in your past, you may consider getting professional help so that you can return to a healthy sexual relationship once again.

Boundaries involving the sex act need to be agreed upon by both partners, not just the addict. For most recovering couples, the growth in your sexuality will seem awkward at first, but in the long run will increase the possibility of a great, mutually enjoyable sex life together. The following check-list my be used by you and your partner. Anything that doesn't have a "yes", by your partner and you would constitute something you will not do during the sex act.

Sexual Behavior	Myself		My Partner	
_____	Y	N	Y	N
_____	Y	N	Y	N
_____	Y	N	Y	N
_____	Y	N	Y	N
_____	Y	N	Y	N
_____	Y	N	Y	N
_____	Y	N	Y	N
_____	Y	N	Y	N

Our mutual boundaries are:

_____   _____

_____   _____

_____   _____

_____   _____

If this boundary is violated, the consequences are:

1st time _____

2nd time _____

3rd time _____

Circle one:

I will make myself accountable to my   therapist.   sponsor.   other _____.

EMPOWERMENT EXERCISE #49

THROWING IT ALL AWAY

The addiction of your partner has created a lot of losses in your lives. You had your picture of happiness, trust, fidelity, and you thought you were the apple of his eye. This addiction has created a large scratch across this picture. You may have suffered sleepless nights, mood swings and incredible confusion as you tried to make sense out of something that made no sense at all. It is for this reason that you come to a place now where you may throw it all away.

What I mean by this is that you are entitled to own every loss that this addiction has brought into you life. On a separate sheet of paper, make a list of as many things you can possibly think of that you lost because of the addiction. Even the secret things that you don't tell anyone about (the constant comparing you do of your self and other women, etc.). Make this list as long as it has to be. This may take some time, so schedule some recovery time for yourself to do this. After you make your list, go ahead and take tablet and write down one loss per sheet of paper. If you had 30 losses, this will take thirty pieces of paper.

Once you have your second list ready, do some form of "throwing away" event for yourself. You can start a fire and burn one at a time or throw one in a garbage can or disposal at a time. Some women have attached each loss to a separate balloon and then let the balloons fly away.
Throwing it away can help you identify some of your real losses, get them out of your head and into a healing process. This is a way of owning these as your losses, allowing the grieving and healing to start so that this disease does not take anything else away from you. You deserve to get better so do something good for yourself and THROW IT AWAY !

EMPOWERMENT EXERCISE #50

GIVING MYSELF PERMISSION

As a partner of a sex addict, you were instantly faced with many painful decisions and feelings when you first found out about your partner's addiction. The largest of these decisions is what to do about your relationship especially if you have been married 10, 20, 30 or more years. In working with many partners across the country, I know that the decision regarding your relationship can appear to be black or white at first. Either you leave as soon as possible or you stay no matter what. This way of thinking about the problem can cause much distress. Let's look at what the options really are.

1. <u>Stay in a sick relationship</u>: The addict is not getting help and it is not going to get better. This doesn't sound like an option but it is. You as the partner just put up with whatever the addict dishes out. The women who choose this option may stay for financial reasons, for the children, or for lack of self-esteem.

2. <u>Divorce</u>: This option for some is taken immediately and for others it is taken after trying everything else and the addict still chooses not to stop the behavior.

3. <u>Separate</u>: This option when used correctly, can be affective. The reasons for separation needs to be written down along with the goals that need to be accomplished by both persons under the accountability of a therapist or pastor. When you revisit, you review the progress or lack thereof until you decide to reunite or divorce. Make sure you make the goals behavioral such as: attend support groups, therapy, etc.

4. <u>Stay together and both work on recovery</u>: This can be done if both partners are mature enough to look at their own issues and focus on solving them individually as well as evaluating the current relationship structure and making the appropriate system changes.

Giving yourself permission during the process of this major life decision is important. Some have found it helpful to write out each case scenario. How would this decision affect me spiritually, sexually, financially, socially and as a parent? At the end of writing out each one of these case scenarios (except stay and stay sick), write a paragraph to yourself giving permission to make this decision. This can unclog pent up feelings and fears that surround each option as you consider what to do with your life from this point forward.

While giving yourself permission, some have found it helpful to give themselves also some time before they follow through with their decision. An example may be to say, "I will decide this in three months from now, and circle the date on the calendar. This gives you time to evaluate the relationship and the progress you both are making. It also gives you time to prepare intelligently for you next step. Giving yourself permission can relax you just enough to make a thoughtful choice that is in your best interest. After all, you are worth taking the time to figure this out.

PART TWO: PERSONAL GROWTH EXERCISES

EMPOWERMENT EXERCISE #51

STEP TWO

"Came to believe a power greater than ourselves could restore us to sanity."

     Coming to believe in one power that is able to heal you is a process. I know from experience that "a power greater than yourself" can, with your active cooperation, do the job of restoration.

     In Step Two, if you have a religious background, this may be a place for you to rediscover a forgotten heritage. For others, you will start with a totally clean slate spiritually and get the joy of discovering for the first time a connecting with a greater power. A more thorough exploration of Step Two is given in the <u>Beyond Love</u> workbook made available in the back of this book.

Behaviors that support Step Two are:

<u>BEHAVIOR</u>	<u>YES</u>	<u>NO</u>
1. Honesty about your spiritual place	_____	_____
2. Prayer	_____	_____
3. Meditation	_____	_____
4. Spiritual reading	_____	_____
5. Dialoguing with others you feel have a God-connection to discover their experiences	_____	_____

EMPOWERMENT
EXERCISE #52

GRIEF

As a partner of a sex addict, you will naturally go through the grieving process. It is helpful for you to understand grief as a process. You will find that at times, grieving will be the reason you are behaving in a peculiar way. You may wonder, "What is wrong with me?" Grieving will probably be the answer, especially in the first six months to a year after discovering this.

Remember, you have already suffered severe losses by the discovery of the addiction in your relationship. Be patient with yourself as you would be to anyone else who has had a significant loss. The different stages of grief are listed below.

SHOCK - This is the moment you realized that you were a partner of a sex addict. This may be accompanied by numbness or a sense of emotional nausea. This stage is usually fleeting and may last minutes, hours or sometimes days.

DENIAL - For the partner, denial can be that you don't believe your spouse has a problem. It can also be applied to denial of partner issues that you may face in your recovery.

ANGER - This is the first stage in which you begin to process that he "may" be a sex addict. You are probably very angry at this realization. "Why?" You may dislike that your partner is an addict, but at least you are finally wrestling with the painful truth. This stage is often accompanied by mood swings, irritability and irrational behavior.

BARGAINING - This is the stage that "He's not an addict if..." The "if" can be "if I can stop him or control him for a while...", or "if I can be enough for him, he will stop," or wishes that "if there was just some magic formula" then we would not have this problem. Bargaining seeks to relieve the sting of the fact that he is a sex addict and it is a very creative stage.

SORROW - This is when it starts hitting you. You are a partner of a sex addict. This may not feel very good, but it is true. You now know there are going to have to be changes. You can feel it. You are sad about the fact that he is a sex addict and what it has done to your life.

ACCEPTANCE - "I am a partner of a sex addict." You now accept his addiction. You are no longer blaming or looking for a magical way to avoid the process of recovery. Your behavior is active in recovery. Your creativity is being used to find time and ways to recover, and you are being honest even when it hurts to be.

In the space below, circle the stage that you believe you are currently in. In a few weeks, check back and see if there is movement. Grief is a process. Being in Grief is okay because if you pass denial, you are actively going through the reality of being a partner of a sex addict.

SHOCK   DENIAL   ANGER   BARGAINING   SORROW   ACCEPTANCE

EMPOWERMENT EXERCISE #53

GRIEVING WHO HE WAS

The person you dated and the person you married both may have been very nice. You were the center of his young world. He was probably full of life, ambition, and dreams. He presented himself maybe as a nice guy, a straight arrow so to speak, or possibly as religious. Then this? He's a what! A sex addict! How can this be? Some had absolutely no clue at all. After all, he is an upstanding member of the community, church, a good father, and you thought up to this point an okay husband as well. For others, the journey had some question marks. There was unaccountable time or money. He has been unavailable during business travels. You may have stumbled upon pornographic magazines, video's, or sex objects and there is the pressure for you to do more sexually.

No matter which journey you have taken, the fact is he's a sex addict. This fact can dramatically change who you though he was. It is especially confusing for the person whose partner played himself as Joe Honest.

Exercise: On a piece of paper, write a good-bye letter to who 1) I thought you were all these years, 2) Who you are now, and 3) Who I thought you were going to be in the future. You may have built much of your life around who you thought he was. It is very important that this loss is grieved in the past, present and future. The sooner you can accept him for who he really is, an addict, which he has been probably since his early teens, the quicker you can get better if he chooses to recover.

My experience with those I counsel is that within six months they are, if sober, nicer than ever in their life. Accepting him is part of your healing. I find you don't try as hard to change those you accept.

EMPOWERMENT EXERCISE #54

GRIEVING THE PICTURE

You probably have a general picture of how your life was when you were a child. You may also have general pictures of what you thought your relationship was as well. These pictures are usually in the past, present, and future.

The **past** picture you thought you lived in can now be fractured by the facts you have learned about certain events, other women, possibly even friends that were involved in your partner's sex addiction. The sense of what you thought was security can now be riddled with confusion and questions.

The **present** picture of "What now? What am I supposed to do? Who do I tell? Who knows?" along with feelings of betrayal or humiliation, cloud a picture that was once pleasant or at least familiar. This addiction robbed you of the familiar picture of what you thought and felt about your relationship. Grieving your present losses is also important.

The **future** held the picture of your lives together, retirement, and friends. Now this also has a cloud of questions hovering over it as well. The future to some is a great loss. It was what both of you worked so hard for. Dreams you thought you were building together may be questionable now that you have found out that he is a sex addict.

This picture of the past, present and future needs to be grieved and processed. You will need to write a letter saying good bye to the picture of the life you thought you had, your present picture and the future that you thought was going to be. To further process this exercise, you may want to read it out loud to your recovery friend or your group.

Every woman has to grieve what was, what is and what you thought was to come. The present and future are definitely going to be different than what you expected. The future for some may be better. If you both work a solid recovery program and deal with past personal issues, you can both experience something great. What I am experiencing is way beyond what I ever could have conceived in my early recovery. Nevertheless we have to grieve what we thought was reality so we can walk in our present reality successfully.

EMPOWERMENT
EXERCISE #55

ANGER LETTER

Imagine putting your addict in a padded room, strapped to a chair, and gagged. He will now have to listen to you. When you would leave, he wouldn't remember a word you said. What would you say?

A lot of you have most likely endured some type of neglect in many areas of your life because of your addicted partner. You may have endured the shame of his behaviors and the losses of relationships because of him. He has probably, in many ways, caused you pain.   You should be angry about this pain and you would be totally justified to this anger since you have been injured.

It is for this reason you need to write an anger letter. This letter is to your addict. To begin writing this letter, you would need to write down all the feelings of anger, rage, hurt and everything you wish you could tell him about what he did. This letter is never to be seen by him. This letter is for your healing not for him to read so he can "feel the pain." I never suggest that your partner read this letter. You can make this letter as long as you need it to be and you can use any language you feel you need to communicate the anger you have. To heal, you must get rid of the anger especially if you intend to stay in this relationship. On a piece of paper, write out what you need to say. Sharing this letter with your recovery friend or group member(s) can be helpful as well.

EMPOWERMENT EXERCISE #56

ANGER WORK

After you have your anger letter completed from the previous exercise, you can do this exercise. Do not do this exercise without doing the anger letter. It will not be nearly as effective.

You will need a bat or solid racket of some kind and a mattress or a pillow for a target before you can start this exercise. It will take about 1-1/2 hours of total alone time, so don't forget to turn off the phones.

First, you warm up by taking the bat/racket and hitting the target with one small hit, then a medium hit and a large hit and a very large hit. Then do the same exercise again but with two small hits, two medium hits, two large hits and two very large hits. Then do the set of hits again but with three hits.

The second part of the warm up includes your voice along with these hits. Use the word "no" in a quiet voice, a medium voice, a loud voice, and an extra loud voice while hitting the mattress or pillow with corresponding hits. Then do two sets of this and then three.

Next, take your anger letter and read it out loud as if he were in the room with you. Lastly, after the reading of the letter, take your bat/racket and hit the target saying the things you said in the letter and anything else that comes to mind. You may cry during the exercise, but this isn't the goal, stay angry during this time and you may get the relief you need.

This exercise usually only needs to be done one time. If you feel you didn't get what you needed or didn't let go of control enough, you can try again. If you feel you need help with this exercise, you can set up a telephone appointment. Instructions are in the back of this workbook for this service.

Anger Work

1. Get equipment and time prepared
2. Warm up:

	1st	2nd	3rd
Small hit	1 hit	2 hits	3 hits
Medium hit	1 hit	2 hits	3 hits
Large hit	1 hit	2 hits	3 hits
Extra large hit	1 hit	2 hits	3 hits

3. Add the voice to above warm up
4. Read letter
5. Hit the bed - Say what you need to say

Warning: If you have any medical conditions, consult your doctor before doing this exercise

EMPOWERMENT
EXERCISE #57

SELF ABANDONMENT

A consistent themes which pops up while I am working with partners of sex addicts is self abandonment. This form of abandonment is usually a gradual process. Slowly, the partner of the addict abandons herself and her needs to stay in her relationship with the sex addict. The forms of abandonment may vary from losing long-term friendships to abandoning her sexuality to the addict.

Self-abandonment must be addressed on the road to recovery. You are worth being taken care of and meeting your own needs. To start this process, let's look at the areas in which you may have abandoned yourself during the course of relating to the addict. Check off the abandonments that apply to you. Share these with your recovery friend or group members.

❑   Abandoning your intuition (when you knew you were right)

❑   Giving up significant relationships

❑   Giving up your spirituality or church

❑   Performing uncomfortable sexual behaviors

❑   Dressing the way he wants you to, instead of the way you feel comfortable

❑   Not pursuing an education

❑   Not being financially aware

❑   No allowing yourself to be cherished, nurtured or celebrated in a relationship

❑   Not allowing yourself to be listened to when trying to communicate

❑   Not allowing yourself goals or dreams

❑   Not developing your own hobbies or interests

❑   Other _____

❑   Other _____

❑   Other _____

❑   Other _____

❑   Other _____

EMPOWERMENT EXERCISE #58

SELF CARE PLAN

A self-care plan is simply a plan to take of yourself. Each person will have different needs that have to be planned out in order to take care of those needs. In the previous exercise you checked off some of the areas of abandonment which applied to you. They will be used for this exercise.

When you identify a need in your life, you will want to make a plan to meet that need. After making your plan to take care of yourself, you may need to actually schedule time for this need to be met. When you have your plan, make it known to your recovery friend or support group. Start off with small goals. Some partners start with giving themselves 15-30 minutes a day to take a long bath or to read a book uninterrupted. Some of the longer term goals (such as education) you may have to break down to weekly or monthly segments.

The areas I want to take care of myself are:

_____   _____

_____   _____

_____   _____

_____   _____

The goal for this week is _____

_____

Have I completed my goal? Why or why not?_____

My goals for this month are: _____

_____

Have I completed my goal? Why or why not?_____

EMPOWERMENT
EXERCISE #59

GUILT

Many partners of sex addicts carry some form of guilt. Some have guilt for staying in the relationship, others have guilt for sexual acts they may have participated in at the sex addict's request. Whatever the reason is that you have guilt, it is important to address this guilt during your recovery. Guilt is a strong emotion and it can paralyze you forcing you to stay in unhealthy relationships. Possibly your partner has threatened to tell or show people what you may have done during your relationship together? Some addicts purposely set their partners up so they can create guilt and shame so they can stay in control of their partners. They may threaten to tell secrets if their partner doesn't stay or continue to perform certain behaviors.

On a piece of paper, list the behaviors or events that you have guilt over in your relationship with a sex addict. Be honest with yourself. These secrets can keep you unhealthy and vulnerable to continue in more unhealthy relationships in your life.

EMPOWERMENT EXERCISE #60

FORGIVING YOURSELF

In the last exercise, you made a list of the behaviors or events that you felt guilty about. In this exercise, you will use that list to forgive yourself. You are often hardest on yourself. Often you may give grace and latitude to other people, yet not to yourself. You are a person of worth and you no longer need to be trapped in this guilt.

You will need two chairs in this exercise. Sit in one chair (chair A) and place the other chair (chair B) in front of you. Siting in chair A, imagine yourself also sitting in chair B. With your list of the things you feel guilty about, ask yourself to forgive you. You can take as long as you need, and list anything else you want to forgive yourself for as well during the conversation.

When you are finished asking yourself for forgiveness, move yourself physically into Chair B. In chair B, you heard a request for forgiveness. Talk to that hurting, vulnerable person. If you decide to forgive her, tell her that. Love her and tell her any other nurturing things you can tell her at this time.

When you are finished forgiving yourself, put yourself physically in chair A and appropriately thank yourself for the forgiveness you have received.

EMPOWERMENT
EXERCISE #61

GOD FORGIVE ME

Partners of sex addicts as we discussed, may have guilt. Through the last two exercises, you were able hopefully to identify this guilt as well as forgive yourself for it.

In the lives of many partners of sex addicts, God is important. If this relationship is important to you and you feel guilt in this relationship, it will be important to rid yourself of the guilt in this relationship to continue to grow spiritually.

As in the last exercise, you will need two chairs. You sit in one chair with your guilt list and figuratively put God in the other chair. You ask God to forgive you and when you are finished asking, switch chairs. This will be the only time you get to actually play God. God being love, already knew and saw this behavior. He feels your pain and wants you free from the guilt so you can be closer to Him. As God in the other chair, talk back to yourself as you have just asked for forgiveness and give yourself God's response. Remember, be gentle, God is!

After God is finished forgiving you and nurturing you, go back to the first chair and appropriately say "Thank you" to God. Many partners find it helpful to clear the air with God this way in their recovery.

EMPOWERMENT
EXERCISE #62

INTIMACY

Compared to the sex addict, most partners appear to be more in touch with their feelings and desire for intimacy. The sex addict is often very immature emotionally. Intimacy can become an issue for the partner of a sex addict when he begins taking his recovery seriously. After he has been sober a few months and has completed the feelings exercise, an interesting thing can occur with the sex addict. He can become intimate!

The partner who wanted intimacy can now be setting up road blocks so that intimacy does not occur. Such road blocks may be criticism, sarcasm, an emotional wall, rage, control and sabotaging potential intimacy. This change of events from the sex addict can and will bring up your intimacy issues, if you have any. If you find yourself pulling back emotionally and spiritually from your mate when he is actively and behaviorally recovering and changing, it is time to discuss this with a recovery friend or the group.

If you are blocking intimacy, do the feeling exercises with your partner, get accountable to your recovery friend or group to allow intimacy to happen. Intimacy is a wonderful thing but only grows when both partners have no agendas, accept each other's faults, and promote skills to be emotionally available and honest. Many partners have never experienced intimacy and may fear it because of the unfamiliarity and the inability to control what happens if you are intimate with your partner or anyone else.

EMPOWERMENT
EXERCISE #63

CONTROL

Control is an illusion. It does not exist when it comes to human beings. You only need to be with a 2 year old for a short time to know that this is true. Control as a defense mechanism does exist. Most partners of sex addicts believe control does exist. Then they make assumptions on how to get and keep their control (manipulation). They may practice different strategies on different people until they find the magic formula and apply this potion at will to any unsuspecting victim. This may sound extreme but I believe this point is well made.

Many partners of sex addicts rightly have insecurities and fears about their relationships and secrets from their past that have not been dealt with and therefore use control as their defense mechanism. When the partner tries to control the addict and determine the outcome, she often is angry or hurt when it doesn't come out the way she planned. Control is sometimes a necessary defense mechanism to survive abuse or a chaotic relationship. Survival is not the goal in recovery, living is. To live fully, we have to eliminate control.

On another piece of paper, you may want to write a thank you and good-bye letter to control. After all, she was there to protect you. She was faithful and should be thanked for carrying you to this point. A second part of losing control is to make a list of the primary people in your life and honestly admit how you tried to control them by anger, shame, criticism, withholding love, sex, praise or affection.

After you make your list, share these with a recovery friend or group member. Then make a goal to be accountable to one person a month on your list of controlling behaviors.

EMPOWERMENT EXERCISE #64

STEP THREE

"Made a decision to turn our life and will over to the care of God as we understood Him."

Making a decision of this magnitude can and should take some time in your recovery process. In Step Two, we were spending time with God, discovering His existence and how this relationship is working out. Much like those who are married, first we dated our spouse and eventually over time, and after experiences, we decided to marry, then followed through with this decision. The decision to marry affected every part of our life: socially, financially, sexually, emotionally, and, in various other areas, redefined us and some of our behaviors. Turning your life over to the care of God is a similar experience. It is walking down the aisle with God, a lifelong commitment to stay in a relationship. This relationship grows over time. The depth of our experience and time together will reinforce our concept of God.

Behaviors that support Step Three are:

	BEHAVIOR	**YES**	**NO**
1.	Prayer	_____	_____
2.	Spiritual reading	_____	_____
3.	Asking God to be involved in every area of your life	_____	_____
4.	Behaviorally follow what you know to be God's will, even when we want it another way	_____	_____

EMPOWERMENT
EXERCISE #65

FIVE YEARS FROM NOW: UNRECOVERED

In your recovery, it is helpful to have a clear counter-picture in your mind to fight this addiction. A clear, practiced picture of what it will be like five years from now without recovery and in an active relationship with an unrecovering sex addict. This picture with the feelings that go with it, can be a helpful tool against this addiction.

On the below lines, write out what you think your life would be like if you didn't stay in recovery and went back to an active sexually addictive relationship. Things to include in your picture are: people you wouldn't be seeing, where you would be living, the condition of your marriage, your relationship with your children, your health, your job, where your career would be going, the risk of disease, amount of time and energy he would spend on his addiction, how you would feel about yourself, your secrets, your spiritual condition and any other situations you can think of to add to your picture.

My life 5 years from now.

_____

_____

_____

_____

_____

_____

_____

Take this picture and practice bringing the picture up with the emotions you have listed above. Having practiced this picture 2 to 3 times a day for 3-5 days can give you a tool to help you get and stay clean.

EMPOWERMENT
EXERCISE #66

PICTURE YOURSELF: UNRECOVERED

In the space provided, draw a picture of yourself in light of five years without recovery.

Describe yourself:

_____

_____

_____

Describe your feelings:

_____

_____

_____

Commit this picture and the feelings to memory. Practice this picture 2 to 3 times daily for 3 to 5 days. This experience can help you counter the "pretty" picture you may have created.

EMPOWERMENT EXERCISE #67

FIVE YEARS FROM NOW: RECOVERING

Another picture that is helpful to combat your situation is the picture of you having a successful recovery and enjoying yourself, your partner, family, career, and other relationships and activities.

As someone who has experienced the positive picture of recovery and living a happy, fulfilling and balanced life, I know this picture helps fight off the desire for old behaviors.

In the space provided below, write out what you think your life would be like with growth in your life of recovery. Things to include would be: friends, career, your marital situation, your relationship with your children, your health, risk of sexual diseases, how you feel about yourself, any secrets, your spiritual condition, recreational interests or hobbies and anything else you can see for yourself in a positive recovery future.

My life in recovery 5 years from now:

_____

_____

_____

_____

_____

_____

_____

My feelings about this picture:

_____

_____

_____

Take this picture and practice it 2 to 3 times a day for 3 to 5 days along with the feelings that go with it. This picture can be yours. After the hard work of recovery, especially in the first year, there is a life that can be as fulfilling as you desire in every area of your life, spiritual, emotional, health, marital, friend, family and even financial. My hope is that you experience this picture. I have, and I know you can, too.

EMPOWERMENT
EXERCISE #68

PICTURE YOURSELF: RECOVERING

In the space below, draw a picture of yourself after five years of successful recovery.

Describe yourself:

_____

_____

_____

_____

Describe your feelings:

_____

_____

_____

_____

Commit this picture to memory along with the feelings you have about it. Practice this among the other pictures daily 2 to 3 times for 3 to 5 days. This can be another positively reinforced picture to keep you in recovery.

EMPOWERMENT
EXERCISE #69

_____

OUR FAMILIES AND THEIR ADDICTIONS

In the field of addiction and recovery from any addiction, whether it be co-dependency, alcohol, drugs, sex or food, we know as a researched phenomenon, that addictions often run in families. In treatment for addiction, you can do what clinicians call a genogram which is another name for a family tree.

This exercise can be made to be complicated by putting down divorces, etc. For purposes of this space, draw your family tree using only first names. Take a different colored pen and write next to each name any addiction you feel this relative may have. A possible list might be: Alcohol, co-dependency, drugs, sex, food, television, nicotine and so on. If you are aware of sexual abuse in your family tree, put an asterisk next to that relative's name as well.

This exercise helps you put addiction in a family context. This often helps you to see that you definitely didn't get where you are by yourself.

In some cases, it can help to look at yourself and your partner more kindly. For many partners and sex addicts, both are probably the first family members with a real opportunity to stop the sexual addiction from going down the family tree any further.

EMPOWERMENT
EXERCISE #70

SEX ADDICTION IN OUR FAMILY

The genogram in the last exercise brought to light those in your family with various addictions including sex addiction. In the spaces below, list those you feel have sexual addiction or codependency issues and why? Secondly, list those who you think were sexually abused in your family tree and why? If you believe no one in your family has had either issue, you may be very fortunate or you just may not have all the information. (Some families keep secrets better than others.)

NAME/RELATIONSHIP   **WHY**

1. _____   _____

2. _____   _____

3. _____   _____

4. _____   _____

5. _____   _____

6. _____   _____

7. _____   _____

8. _____   _____

9. _____   _____

10. _____   _____

In specifically looking at sexual addiction and abuse, you can sometimes see generationally how this addiction has been carried through out the family. In my family, sex addiction and sexual abuse occurred on both sides of my family tree. This realization is much like those that were early in recovery from alcoholism in the 1930s. They knew it was in the family, but the knowledge about the disease wasn't available. The support groups were not there, and there certainly was not a book like the one you are reading that could help them step by step to choose recovery. Many in their family history had little choice of recovery or healing from sexual addiction. Write down what are your thoughts and feelings about possibly being the first in your family to be able to even choose recovery.

EMPOWERMENT
EXERCISE #71

MY SEXUAL HISTORY

A sexual history is something that many partners have stored in their minds. It is the faces, pictures and events that periodically come into your thoughts. These pictures sometimes stir up feelings of all different kinds. In your recovery, you may be less than proud of your sexual history. Regardless of where you are in your recovery, your sexual history can be a tool to help you see and discover things about yourself.

To do a sexual history, get a pen and paper and simply go through your life in increments of 5 years (1-5, 6-11, 12-17, 18-23...). Write down your sexual experiences. This would include exposure to pornography at various ages, masturbation patterns, sexual abuse, rape, forced encounters in your marriage and your first sexual experience. This history when done thoroughly, will help you when you complete your Fourth Step. The temptation will be to not be entirely honest. If you hit an experience like this, you can write it down so that others may not understand it. The types of sex you experienced are part of your history. You are to some degree shaped by these experiences. Also, you may want to put an asterisk by those who you believe were sex addicts. Some partners have realized patterns of mostly being with sex addicts. Some have even acknowledged that they have never known sexual intimacy with anyone.

A complete history will have several benefits such as:

1.   It is finally all out.
2.   Great progress toward Fourth Step.
3.   You will now be able to complete the sex cycles exercise.

EMPOWERMENT
EXERCISE #72

SEX CYCLES

In the previous exercise, you took great courage to write down your entire sexual history. This is important and can help you identify patterns in your sexual experiences and the partners with whom you were sexual.

Some review their sexual histories and find a series of re-victimizations, or that their first sexual experience was abusive and that they were used as an object. You may also find out something about those you chose to be sexual with, such as they were emotionally unavailable or that they were unfaithful to you. A pattern of being unfulfilled sexually and seeking the magic fix can also emerge. Stress and financial pressure for some are related to sexual cycles. There is also the sex cycle of reward and punishment that some partners get into with the addict in order to try to control his behavior. Some have noticed cycles of increased sexual activity after a new disclosure or finding out about the addict's behavior. There are a myriad of possible sexual cycles. In the below space, briefly write out the cycles you recognize in your sexual history.

_____

_____

_____

_____

Now that you have identified some cycles as they relate to your sexual history, you may for the first time realize the reality of certain cycles or patterns in your past or current relationships. To make the most of these realizations, it will help if you make a plan or strategy to "short circuit" the patterns that are already in place.

_____

_____

_____

_____

EMPOWERMENT EXERCISE #73

TYPES OF SEX

The types of sex listed below are taken from the book *Women Who Love Sex Addicts*. This approach can help you to see the type of sex you have had primarily with your partner(s). The sex addict is often amazed that after 5-10 or more years of objectifying or maybe masturbation sex, that his partner isn't interested that much in sex. Many sex addicts and their partners have rarely even had relational sex in their entire sexual experience. Some couples are experiencing sexual anorexia, the avoidance of intimacy and sex.

The awareness of the types of sex can help you to aim for personable sex in your recovery as well as give insight into the type of sex you have been experiencing with your partner. In recovery, you can have a growing sexual relationship that is not only personal but nurturing and fulfilling as well.

Relational Sex: Both partners enjoy each other as a person, and are able to communicate sexual needs to one another. One or both partners may or may not have an orgasm, but both have a sense of nurturing each other. Sex is not the focus or the priority in this relationship.

Physical Sex: This is where one or both partners enjoy primarily the physical act, but still the relationship is not threatened. This type of sex may happen to all couples eventually. There's not much feeling, but there is no shame either.

Objectifying Sex: This type of sex may or may not be pleasurable to one partner, but the other one is fantasizing about other acts with this same partner. One person's orgasm is the focus of this sexual act. The other partner may or may not feel that they are important to the orgasmic partner.

Masturbating Sex: One partner is fantasizing about other partner, pornographic movies, books, or someone of the same sex, while having sex with his partner. The fantasy is the excitement that leads to the person of focus having an orgasm, not his partner. The partner may feel used, absent, or resentful of this sexual encounter.

Violating Sex: This is where one partner demands from his partner certain behaviors. She does not feel comfortable in doing them, but she complies, hoping he will stop nagging her for this sexual act. The partner feels violated as a person, and may have anger or resentment toward her partner for insisting they do this activity.

Traumatizing Sex: The partner is forced physically or with the threat of a weapon or physical pain, to perform a sexual act with her partner. This constitutes rape, and the woman may feel incredible fear of the perpetrator, as well as feelings of victimization and trauma.

EMPOWERMENT
EXERCISE #74

SEXUAL SYSTEMS

As couples evolve together, they create systems for various aspects of their relationship such as who manages the money, who takes the children to school, and who takes out the garbage. Some couples create shared systems or systems may evolve where in one area, one person has total responsibility.

In sex addiction, it is not uncommon for the sex addict, who may initiate sex more frequently than his partner, to end up being totally responsible for the sexual relationship. This leads to discussions to his partner such as "you never initiate sex." Her response may be "you never give me time to." This also leads to the fact that if the addict does all the initiating, he is receiving 100% of the rejections to be sexual no matter how few times this may actually be.

Systems as they evolve with couples, happen slowly and over time. The system around sex is rarely discussed and hence usually does not change. Some of the different sex systems that can be created are listed below.

1. Solo System - Only one person initiates sex, takes all the risk and receives all the refusals. This system can lead to only one person's sexual needs being held as being important.

2. Scheduled System - The couple decides the frequency of sex they want, whether it be once or several times a week, and a particular partner initiates sex on certain nights.

3. Shared System - Both partners are equally responsible for the sexual initiating. The couple decides how to break this up by days, weeks or months.

4. Rotating System - In this system, both partners are responsible to initiate. The couple chooses a frequency of sexual encounters in a week or month and then rotate who is responsible to initiate. For example: James and Robin choose to have sex twice a week. They decide to rotate who initiates on a 3 day schedule. When it is James's turn to initiate, he has three days to manage a convenient time for both of them. When he has initiated, the next day begins Robin's turn to initiate. Neither partner has to wait till the last day to initiate. Couples like this system because they feel more opportunities to be spontaneous within the system.

In the above mentioned systems, it is not uncommon during the development for one or both partners to be aggressive or passive/aggressive in an attempt to resist the change. Some addicts don't like giving up total control of their sex lives and some partners don't want any sexual responsibility. If this occurs, a system of consequences may be set up for the system you both select. This can be a very sensitive topic. You may need some professional guidance in this area to come to an agreed upon system and to create consequences or a sense of guidance as you go through this process.

EMPOWERMENT EXERCISE #75

SEXUAL ASSERTIVENESS

For some, sexual assertiveness may seem to be an oxymoron. In the sex addict's addiction, he may have been sexually aggressive, passive or manipulative, but rarely assertive. The sex addict being sexually aggressive and demanding, or sometimes forcing his sexual demands on you is not healthy and can leave life-long scars. The sexually passive sex addict usually takes care of his own sexual needs through being sexual with himself or being involved in sexual activity outside the relationship. While this is going on, he may avoid your sexual needs. Depriving you of your sexual needs also is unhealthy. Usually in this passive system, you have had to initiate the sexual encounter.

The sex addict is often sexually manipulative. In this arrangement, hints, winks, massages, touches or a sexual comment is supposed to be interpreted by the partner as "I would like to have sex with you." Since these hints or comments are not direct, they can be misunderstood and hence the addict goes away mad because he thought you should be able to read his mind by his manipulations toward sex. This system leaves a lot to interpretation and can lead to many of "you knew what I meant" arguments about sex.

Sexual assertiveness includes two aspects. The first aspect is asking directly to be sexual with your partner. The second aspect is having respect for your partner and realizing that just because you asked or were asked, doesn't mean you are entitled to what you asked for.

To practice sexual assertiveness, ask your partner to sit in a chair in front of you and simply practice several times asking directly to be sexual. Remember this is just a practice. Do not initiate sex at this time otherwise it may feel manipulative. In this exercise, it is not necessary for your partner to have any response. After you have asked several times, switch and allow your partner to ask you the same question. Remember this is a practice exercise. Responding in an inappropriate manner may block the progress this exercise can give you. This exercise can be practiced once or twice a day until both partners feel comfortable asking the other to be sexual. Statements that have worked for other couples are as follows.

- ❑ I would like to be sexual with you, would that be convenient for you?
- ❑ I am feeling sexual and would like to be sexual with you, can we do this?
- ❑ Can we be sexual together?
- ❑ Is being sexual with you an option today or tonight?

NOTE: Do not practice this exercise in the bedroom or at a time you would normally have sex.

EMPOWERMENT EXERCISE #76

REJECTION DESENSITIZATION
(Learning to Say "No")

For the sex addict, the word "no" when it relates to sex with their partner, can create a really big problem. This problem has a long history and an explainable origin. In most of the sex addict's fantasy and masturbation habits from early adolescence until the present, rarely does he hear the word "no." This distorted reality that every time he wanted to ejaculate and had an object (not you) that was willing to accommodate him, caused distorted conditioning. In reality, healthy partners may not want sex every single time they are asked. After clocking in hundreds of hours confirming the sex addict's fantasy with an ejaculation, he really believes that the fantasy is reality.

This is what causes the sex addict to blow up and get so mad or go for long drives to find ways to possibly "get even" when you says "no, not tonight." Some sex addicts go into total rages when rejected sexually. The sex addict's conditioning is the problem, not you.

When you say "No, not tonight," the addict may be hearing "I hate you." The sex addict distorts what she is saying, and it is not reality. This is why it is important to do some desensitization to realize that you are not rejecting him as a person (core belief of a sex addict is that you are your sex), but rather you are just not wanting to participate sexually at this particular time.

Do this exercise at a time you would not normally have sex and preferably not in the bedroom. You and your partner sit face to face, maintaining eye contact. You ask your partner if you can be sexual with him (see assertiveness exercise). He is to have three responses which are noted below.

YOU		PARTNER'S RESPONSE
Would you like to be sexual?	1.	Yes, I would like to have sex with you.
Would you like to be sexual?	2.	I would like to be sexual at a later time.
Would you like to be sexual?	3.	No, I'm not wanting to be sexual at this time.

Practice this several times in one setting with you asking a total of nine times. Then switch and have your partner ask and you will give the responses above. This exercise will probably have to be done 10 to 14 times to get some level of desensitization.

List below the dates you have practiced this exercise:

_____ _____ _____ _____   _____ _____ _____ _____

_____ _____ _____ _____   _____ _____ _____ _____

EMPOWERMENT EXERCISE #77

SEX TALK

During sexual encounters with your partner, it is not uncommon for sex addicts to disconnect and go into various levels of fantasy states (not all do this with their primary partner). As you recover and want a healthier and more satisfying sex life, it is important that you nurture and communicate relationally with each other during your sexual act. The response I so often get from sex addicts and their partners is "what do I say while being sexual?" Below is a list of relational statements that may help you through this dilemma.

☐ I love you.

☐ I really have more love for you now than ever.

☐ Thank you for sharing yourself with me.

☐ You're a terrific lover.

☐ I enjoy being with you.

☐ I feel close to you.

☐ I desire just you.

☐ I'm glad I'm with you.

☐ I'm proud of you.

☐ I love looking at you.

☐ You are such a comfort to me.

☐ I like growing with you.

☐ I love my life with you.

☐ I thank God your my partner.

☐ Thank you for loving me.

☐ You are a great person.

☐ I like you.

☐ I'm glad I married you.

☐ You are handsome.

☐ I love your eyes.

EMPOWERMENT EXERCISE #78

SEX TIPS

During your transformation from objectifying sex to relational sex, there are some tips that may help the process go easier. These tips are for you to practice during your sexual encounters to make it more fulfilling for both partners.

Tip #1 <u>Keep Your Eyes Open</u> - Keeping your eyes open during intercourse makes disconnecting and fantasizing for both partners more difficult. This disconnecting is the first step to fantasy. Being present emotionally during sex may be uncomfortable at first but will become easier as you both practice.

Tip #2 <u>Keep the Lights On</u> - Having some light on during your sexual encounter helps. You can keep eye contact with your partner better if the light is on.

Tip #3 <u>Relational Conversation</u> - Having relational conversation (i.e., I love you. You are handsome.) will also keep you in the present sexual encounter. Stay away from inappropriate talk. Although familiar to may sex addicts and their partners, it may reinforce the addictive, objectifying sex as opposed to reinforcing relational sex with your partner.

EMPOWERMENT EXERCISE #79

PROFESSIONAL COUNSELING

Several different types of counselors are available. Few professionals in the mental health field are aware of or are familiar with sexual addiction treatment at this time. Even fewer are familiar with the issues of partners of sex addicts. Questions to ask those who you would consider for counseling are at the end of this exercise. You may want to consider our counseling services mentioned in the back of this book. For those not living within the local area, our services include telephone counseling, as well.

Along the path of recovery, it may be important or necessary for you to get professional help. This can be a scary enough reality for you. To find someone who is qualified in the area of sexual addiction is essential if the counseling is going to be beneficial to you. Unsuccessful stories of what untrained counselors have told people trying to recover from sex addiction is astounding. Many partners have been told to "just give him more of what he wants."

This is why we have prepared some questions to ask your therapist or doctor before you agree to see him or her. First it is important to note that Psychiatrists are medical doctors whose primary solution for their client is medication. Psychologists, social workers, and master level counselors are more counseling oriented in their solutions for their clients. The questions you may want to ask are:

1. How much experience do you have working with partners of sexual addicts?
2. How much of your practice is related to sexual addiction?
3. Do you have specialized training, certification or licensure in the field of addictions?
4. Are you a recovering person who has worked the 12 Steps personally?
5. What books have you read related to sex addiction and their partners?
6. Do you have specific training dealing with sexual abuse issues?

These six questions can be a starter for you to assess the professional you desire to hire to help you recover from your sexual addiction. It is possible however in your geographical area, to not have a therapist who specializes in sexual addiction or partner's issues.

EMPOWERMENT
EXERCISE #80

STEP FOUR

"Made a searching and fearless inventory of ourselves."

Making an inventory of yourself is helpful in many ways. First, an inventory tells you what has happened and when it happened, both good and harmful. Second, this inventory will give you insight into patterns or cycles of unhealthy behavior. Without this "spreadsheet" you would not be able to see clearly. There are several ways to complete a Fourth Step, but all include in one way or another, writing it down.

Let's define a few terms first such as the word "good" which indicates positive things that happened. "Bad" will mean things that you did that were wrong and you did them any way. "Ugly" will be things that happened to you that you weren't responsible for such as car accidents, surgeries, parent's divorce, abuse or neglect (especially from your sex addicted partner). With these terms in mind, take a piece of paper and draw your columns and a place for the span of your years as seen below and fill in "the rest of the story." Below are some examples.

YEARS	GOOD	BAD	UGLY
1-5			placed in foster home
6-10	won spelling bee		
11-15		had sex when I didn't want to with Fred	
16-20...			

Behaviors that support a Step Four are as follows.

BEHAVIOR		YES	NO
1.	Consistent time spent writing your story	_____	_____
2.	Complete honesty on your story	_____	_____

EMPOWERMENT
EXERCISE # 81

STEP FIVE

"Admitted to God, ourselves, and to another human being the exact nature of our wrongs."

In Step Four, you provided yourself with all the information you need to do Step Five. Step Four is "your" story. This story needs to be admitted to yourself which usually happens during the writing and reading, of your Fourth Step.

"Admitting to God," for some has been an event all by itself. God already knows, but something can happen when you tell Him where you have been. Some visually put God in an empty chair and read their story to Him. This may be a helpful exercise to do in your Fifth Step process.

"Another human being" is by far the toughest part. To allow someone else in is difficult but entirely necessary for your recovery. Pick a person in your recovery program, a support person, or a therapist to share your story with.

The Fifth Step is a must in your recovery. On the other side of doing your Fifth Step, you may feel less guilt and shame and experience true acceptance.

Behaviors that support a Fifth Step are as follows.

BEHAVIORS	**YES**	**NO**
1. A written down Fourth Step	_____	_____
2. A time of reflecting with yourself "admitting to yourself"	_____	_____
3. A time you and God go through "admitting to God"	_____	_____
4. Picking someone to share your Fifth Step with	_____	_____
5. Making an appointment to share "your story"	_____	_____
6. Sharing your Story	_____	_____

The day I completed my Fifth Step was _____.

EMPOWERMENT EXERCISE #82

THE GOSPEL

In my experience of working with recovering partners of sex addicts, I have seen the Gospel as a tool in the lives of those who recover. This experience with the Gospel can give a new life and energy into your recovery. I have seen partners use the Gospel in conjunction with the hard work of doing many of the exercises in this book and receive and maintain the precious gift of recovery as well as a closer walk with God and the eternal life He can give through His son Jesus Christ.

The Gospel is simple. Adam sinned. Christ died for our sins. Receive His forgiveness and become a restored daughter of God. To do this, all you need to do is from your heart, ask God to forgive you and tell Him you accept Christ's death for you so you can be forgiven. He will forgive you and will restore you. I have seen it happen so often that it is a valid tool of recovery.

This is not religion but an invitation into a spiritual relationship. This relationship is one filled with love, acceptance and availability to you. If you say this prayer and want to know more about Christ, you can read the Gospel of John in the New Testament of the Bible. You may want to join others who have experienced this love in a local church that is a healthy example of Christ's love and acceptance.

EMPOWERMENT EXERCISE #83

HIV TEST

The reality of AIDS is everywhere. As a partner of a sex addict, you definitely need to be aware of your possible risk. If the sex addict's behaviors have included other people, you definitely need an AIDS test. This is for your piece of mind. This test can be done anonymously in most of the larger cities in our country. The results take any where from a couple of days to a couple of weeks.

The exercise of getting an AIDS test has brought some soberness to many addicts and their partners if they get tested as well. There is nothing quite like a community clinic to bring home how your addictive partner's life has become out of control and how very much you have to lose if you continue in this relationship without placing the addiction in recovery.

If you need added support to go through this exercise, recruit a recovering person to go to the clinic with you both times. This exercise can also give tremendous relief when the results are consistently negative. Some partners of addicts have requested that the addict do this since he acted out. Even if he does get tested and is negative, you may want to get tested for your own sense of safety.

If you are not sure about your partner's sexual behavior outside of the marriage, then consider a testing for a full battery of sexually transmitted diseases. Your physician can do this for you and assist you if there are other health issues to be looked into.

EMPOWERMENT EXERCISE #84

GROWING UP

Growing Up Sexually

While growing up in your family, you learned a lot of things. Some of these things were helpful and some things you learned at home were not so helpful. This exercise is going to focus on your family's sexual education. As children and adolescents, you are taught not only by what your parents say and do but also the attitudes and unwritten rules your parents believed.

In the area of sex, what did you learn from:

Mom: _____

_____

_____

Dad: _____

_____

_____

From the above information, what beliefs or behaviors have you duplicated in your life? If so, list them below:

_____

_____

_____

What were the long-term results of these beliefs or behaviors about sex that you saw in your parent's life or relationship?

_____

_____

What specific plans can you make to <u>not</u> duplicate these same results in your life and relationships?

_____

_____

_____

How Women are Treated

How you treat yourself and others is usually to some degree what you have seen or experienced in your family of origin. A client I saw recently discovered after 40 years that she created the exact non-intimate relationship that her parents had and that her personal way of relating had a great deal to do with this.

Patterns of relating to your partner are taught by your perceptions of your parents relationship. This can definitely be the case in what you learned about treating your partner. In the spaces below, write what beliefs and behaviors you learned from each person about how women are to be treated:

Dad: _____

_____

Mom: _____

_____

From the above lists, are there any beliefs or behaviors you have duplicated in your life? If so list them below.

_____

_____

What were the long term results of these beliefs or behaviors about how women are treated?

_____

_____

What specific plan can you make not to duplicate these results in your life and relationships?

_____

_____

Growing Up With Anger

Anger is one thing few people talk about. You will need to discuss and deal with anger from several perspectives. In this section, you will be focussing on what you learned about anger from your parents. In some families, you can only discuss feelings after you get mad. In other words, it is okay to hit or be verbally abusive if you are mad. Many rules about anger are learned in the home such as don't get mad, ever. Instead, eat or drink alcohol to cope with your anger, run away, withdraw or emotionally punish others with your anger. In the below space, list what beliefs and behaviors you learned about anger from:

Mom: _____

_____

Dad: _____

_____

From the above list, are there any beliefs or behaviors you have duplicated in your life? If so, list them:

_____

_____

What were the long term results of these beliefs or behaviors about anger that you saw in your parent's life-style or relationship?

_____

_____

What specific plan can you make not to duplicate these results in your life-style and relationship?

_____

_____

EMPOWERMENT
EXERCISE #85

MY RELATIONSHIP WITH DAD

In the space provided, describe your relationship with your dad as you remember it <u>as a child</u> in his house.

_____

_____

_____

_____

In the below space, write about your relationship with your dad as you remember it <u>as a teenager</u>.

_____

_____

_____

In the below space provided, describe your relationship with your dad <u>as an adult</u>.

_____

_____

_____

I feel happy about my dad's relationship because _____

_____

_____

I feel sad about my dad's relationship because _____

_____

_____

I feel mad about my dad's relationship because _____

_____

_____

My wishes for our relationship are _____

_____

_____

_____

Write a letter to your dad. This letter is for therapeutic purposes only. It is not to be sent to him or seen by him unless you discuss it with your sponsor or therapist.

Date I finished my letter: _____

At different times in your recovery, you will need to confront specific issues. The work you have done in the last few pages may have been difficult and emotional. Your courage to be honest will be a great asset in your recovery.

To confront some of these family of origin issues, it is not necessary that you actually go see your parents and drag up all the stuff that you have been processing over many days and sometimes years and try to dump it on them in a one-time conversation. Dumping on them doesn't have to occur for you to get better or even to confront the past issues. What you are about to do may be also difficult and emotional. If you feel you may need support by a recovering person or therapist, please get it.

Take the "Dear Dad" letter that you wrote and sit in a chair with another chair facing you. You can place of picture of your dad on a chair facing you if you want. When you are ready, take your letter to Dad, read it as if he were right there in the chair across from you. You may or may not experience a wide variety of feelings during this exercise.

This empty chair exercise can further your sense of expression toward your dad as well as give you a sense of confronting past feelings or issues. Having these issues addressed can leave you less vulnerable in your present relationship.

EMPOWERMENT
EXERCISE #86

─────────────

MY RELATIONSHIP WITH MOM

In the space provided, describe your relationship with your mom as you remember it <u>as a child.</u>

_____

_____

_____

In the space below, write down what your relationship with your mom was like <u>as a teenager.</u>

_____

_____

_____

In the space provided below, describe your relationship with your mom <u>as an adult.</u>

_____

_____

_____

I feel happy about my relationship with Mom because _____

_____

I feel sad about my relationship with Dad because _____

_____

I feel mad about my relationship with Mom because _____

_____

My wishes about our relationship are _____

_____

_____

On a separate piece of paper, write a letter to your mother. This letter is for therapeutic purposes only and is not to be sent to her or seen by her unless you run it by a therapist or your sponsor. You can express any feelings or situations in your letter and it can be much longer than the space provided.

Date I finished this letter: _____

This exercise is similar to the empty chair exercise you did for Dad. Take your "Dear Mom" letter and sit in a chair with another chair facing you. When you are ready, take your letter to Mom and read it as if she were sitting across from you. You may or may not experience a wide variety of feelings during this exercise.

This empty chair can further your sense of expression toward mom as well as give you a sense of confronting past feelings or issues. Having these issues addressed can leave you less vulnerable in your present relationship.

EMPOWERMENT EXERCISE #87

MY RELATIONSHIP WITH GOD

Now here is some one you may or may not have met growing up. In your family, your parents may have made God important in a healthy way, important in a religiously unhealthy way, occasionally important (i.e.: holidays and emergencies) or not important at all. No matter what your families did or did not do to introduce you to God, many have their own unique development with God.

In this exercise, you will want to look at what you learned about God from your parents. In the spaces below, describe what you believe to be your parent's belief and behaviors about God.

Mom's belief and behaviors about God: _____

_____

_____

Dad's belief and behaviors about God: _____

_____

_____

From the above information, are there any of either or both parents beliefs or behaviors that you have duplicated in your life? If so, what are they?

_____

_____

_____

What were the long-term effects of these beliefs or behaviors (good or bad) that you saw in your parents life or relationship?

_____

_____

_____

What specific plan can you make not to have these negative results in your life and relationship?

_____

_____

In the space below, describe your relationship with God <u>as a child:</u>

_____

_____

_____

In the space below, describe your relationship with God <u>as a teenager:</u>

_____

_____

_____

In the space below, describe your relationship with God <u>as an adult:</u>

_____

_____

_____

Describe your relationship with God as an adult prior to your recovery:

_____

_____

_____

In the space provided below, describe your relationship with God as a recovering person:

_____

_____

_____

On a separate piece of paper, write a letter to God.

Date I wrote this letter: _____

  Since we all come from a variety of backgrounds, God may be different for all of us. In the past pages dealing with family of origin issues, you sat both Mom and Dad symbolically in a chair in front of you and confronted the issues you felt you had with your parents.

  In this exercise, you will do the same confronting of issues with God. God can be a big relationship in your past as well as in your recovery. To have a place where you allow yourself to be open before God is for some, very important in order to move further into your spirituality and relationship with God.

  In light of this, take your "Dear God" letter and place yourself in a chair with a chair in front of you. Read your letter to God and anything else you feel impressed to say to Him. This exercise for some may be difficult and full of a wide variety of emotions. If you feel you need the support of a recovering person or a therapist please provide this for yourself.

EMPOWERMENT EXERCISE #88

ABUSES AND NEGLECTS

During your Fourth Step, you made a column titled "Ugly." In this section of your Fourth Step, you listed events that happened to you that were not your fault although they still impacted your life. It is now time to look at these events and begin recovery from them as part of your recovery.

Many have experienced various forms of abuses growing up. Some emotional abuse instances could consist of being shamed or yelled at regularly, being cut down or humiliated. Emotional neglect could consist of not being talked to, nurtured or cared for, or asked as to how you felt. Physical abuse for some is the hitting or watching others being hit. Physical neglect would include being improperly clothed, not having food for a length of time, and inadequate shelter. Spiritual abuse is sometimes being emotionally or physically abused while your parents justify this by their religious beliefs. Some sexual abuse instances would include exposure to pornography, verbal sexual innuendos, sexual touches, and any sexual behaviors between siblings or parents. Sexual neglect is not informing you about your body changes and about sex.

In the space provided below, check the areas of abuse and or neglects you feel you have experienced:

ABUSES		NEGLECTS	
Emotional	_____	Emotional	_____
Physical	_____	Physical	_____
Spiritual	_____	Spiritual	_____
Sexual	_____	Sexual	_____

EMPOWERMENT
EXERCISE #89

MY PERPETRATORS

In the previous exercise, you took a look at the abuses and neglects you experienced during your growing up years. In this exercise, you are going to look at the people who were involved in these abuses and neglects.

I know at this point, you may be going into extremely painful territory. So painful that many of these issues may be the pain you were medicating for many years. It is important for your recovery and continued growth that you look at these abuses and neglects that you suffered.

In many of the incidences that you have experienced, you may have known the perpetrator's name. For some, these events happened in your own home by parents, stepparents, siblings or extended family. In other cases, there may be a casual relationship that preceded the abuse (i.e. a school teacher, another child at school, or neighbor). You may not know the perpetrator's name. Maybe it happened once and you never saw that person again.

Whatever the name or relationship was, these events have been indelibly written into your life. Now it is time to write down your perpetrator's name (if known), relationship (if any), and the type of abuse that occurred and an approximate age that abuse/neglect happened.

NAME/RELATIONSHIP   ABUSE   AGE

_____

_____

_____

_____

_____

_____

_____

_____

_____

EMPOWERMENT EXERCISE #90

WHAT THEY DID TO ME

What you may have experienced from your perpetrator(s) has probably left pain for many years. This pain is often free-floating inside of you. You may rarely or never talk about what exactly happened, and so it may remain like an emotional blob of gel that you don't seem to have crystallized inside.

In your recovery, it will be important to have these pains you have been medicating all these years to be as crystallized as possible. This will be helpful for you to identify what exactly happened and later to process your feelings about these events.

In this exercise, you will do exactly that: crystallize the memory. In the previous page, you wrote down your perpetrators and their general offences. It is now time to get specific. On a separate paper, list the perpetrator at the top of the page and write down in as much detail as you possibly can exactly what your perpetrator did.

If you have experienced sexual or physical abuse as well as other abuses, this will be painful. If you need the support of others, please call and invite others into this healing process with you. If you feel you need professional help at this point, consider a therapist who specializes in this area of recovery.

EMPOWERMENT EXERCISE #91

RANKING MY PERPETRATOR(S)

Ranking your perpetrator may seem like an odd thing to do, after all, any abuse of no matter what kind should not ever be experienced by anybody. I know this as well as anyone. And in ranking, you are not trying to minimize in any way the pain each perpetrator has inflicted in your life.

I compare the exercise process before you to a battle surgeon. Every wound that a soldier has is painful and wrong and yet some wounds will require different levels of procedures and some wounds may demand more attention than others. It is my experience that in the letter and anger work ahead, it is best to proceed by ranking the perpetrators by our perception as to who has caused more damage and pain so you can outline a surgery plan.

In the next exercises, you will need to list the perpetrators that you have ranked as less severe than others so as to work up to the major trauma that will require a lot from you as an injured person. In practicing with these in a ranked order, you will be stronger and know the process and what to expect a lot better as you move into the higher ranked trauma events.

On the previous page where you listed your perpetrators, the abuse/neglect and their age, write in next to their name a rank, starting with #1 as the least offending to the most severe as the highest numbered abuse.

EMPOWERMENT EXERCISE #92

LETTER(S) TO MY PERPETRATOR(S)

This exercise takes you a step further into healing from your abuses and/or neglects that you may have experienced. Much like you have already done in creating letters to help you resolve some of the family of origin issues, you must now write a letter to help heal these areas of abuse and neglect.

This letter to each of your perpetrators is for therapeutic purposes, not to be sent to the perpetrator(s). These letters are for your recovery, not theirs. It is important for you to confront the issues and not necessarily the person, especially not at this point of your healing and recovery. You may have a wide range of feelings as you do this exercise. You may want to solicit the help of a recovering person and stay in closer touch with your group during this time.

In this exercise, write a letter you would read to your perpetrator. Imagine he was strapped to a chair and couldn't say anything back to you. You can say anything and everything you want to say. This letter can be full of hate, anger, disgust and many other powerful emotions. You can use any language necessary to express yourself. These events should have never happened, so your feelings are totally appropriate.

These letters can be as long as you need to fully express yourself. These letters can bring up past feelings and memories. Give yourself permission to feel and take as much time as you need. You are worth the time and energy you will spend on your letters.

Now write down the perpetrator you ranked least on the previous page, and begin to write your letter. After you write your letter, you may want to do an empty chair exercise and read your letter to the perpetrator. If you feel you need extra support, please give this gift to yourself.

If after reading the letter, you feel a sense of resolve, great. If you feel there is more work to do then you may want to consider doing the anger exercise mentioned earlier in this workbook.

EMPOWERMENT
EXERCISE #93

STEP SIX

"Were entirely ready to have God remove all these defects of character."

Defects of character may be more obvious to you now that you have written and acknowledged your story to God, yourself and another human being. In Step Six, you can begin to see some of your limitations or things that are less than positive about yourself. Before you can become "entirely ready," it has been helpful to take some reflective time and list your defects of character. In no particular order, writing down your defects (i.e.: impatient, manipulative, selfish) helps you to know what it is that you are getting ready to have God remove.

The simplest way to do this, is to list in the left hand column your character defects. Next to each character defect, write the percentage of willingness to have God remove this defect, (EXAMPLE: Selfishness - 75%). Review your list regularly until there is a 100% next to each defect. During the starting of this list and it's completion you may want to pray over those areas that are less than 100%.

Behaviors supporting a Step Six are as follows:

BEHAVIORS	**YES**	**NO**
1. A list made of "defects of character"	——	——
2. A regular review until 100% "entirely ready"	——	——
3. Prayer during the process of becoming "entirely ready"	——	——
4. Discussions about defects taking longer to be "entirely ready"	——	——

Date I became "entirely ready" to have God remove my defects of character _____.

EMPOWERMENT EXERCISE #94

STEP SEVEN

"Humbly asked Him to remove our shortcomings."

You may be very familiar with your shortcomings. Familiarity can sometimes make it difficult to get into a humble place and ask God to remove them. In my life, my shortcomings hurt those I loved very much and looking back, these same shortcomings also hurt me. Shortcomings, for many recovering people, need a real miracle to be removed.

I liken this process to that of your child, parent, or spouse who might suddenly be diagnosed with a cancer or other life threatening disease and all the doctor had to say is "if you pray, now is a good time to do so." Many people, regardless of their life-history or circumstances, would muster up a "humbly asking" position before God. If someone was watching you, they might call it begging, pleading for him to be merciful "just this once." This is the sort of place that is most helpful to be while completing your Seventh Step.

Asking God to remove your shortcomings in light of what you just discussed, is hard spiritual work. While working on your Step Seven, you may want to seriously consider completing just one or two defects a day. More than this may be too draining or may be minimizing this defect. Some have found it helpful to write down a paragraph or two about how this defect of character has hurt them as well as others in order to assist them to humbly ask God to remove them.

Behaviors that support a Step Seven are as follows.

BEHAVIORS	**YES**	**NO**
1. List of defects	_____	_____
2. Paragraph on how defects affect you and those you love.	_____	_____
3. A reflective time	_____	_____
4. A prayer time for each defect	_____	_____

Date I completed praying over each defect _____.

EMPOWERMENT EXERCISE #95

STEP EIGHT

"Made a list of all persons we have harmed and became willing to make amends to them all."

This step is still another one that involves pen and paper. This step is quite straight forward. List on a piece of paper those you feel you harmed.

After you make your list, put a percentage next to it representing how currently ready you are to make an amend to this person, (i.e. Sue - 75%). Review your list regularly until all people on your list have 100% next to them. This exercise may take prayer and reflection until all people have a 100% next to their name. This Step is just to move us to be "willing."

Behaviors that support Step Eight are as follows.

BEHAVIORS	**YES**	**NO**
1. A list of persons harmed	_____	_____
2. Percentages that increase to 100%	_____	_____
3. Prayer and reflection	_____	_____
4. Discussion with support people over difficult issues	_____	_____

EMPOWERMENT
EXERCISE #96

STEP NINE

"Made direct amends to such people wherever possible, except when to do so would injure them or others."

This step takes into consideration those to whom your direct amends "may" injure. This part of the step is not a loophole so that you don't have to make amends to someone. If you feel you have such a situation, tell the situation to two people who have done their Step Eight and/or a therapist and if they agree with you, then this is probably a legitimate situation not to give an amend.

The rest of this step is quite simple, with the list you have in Step Eight, write next to each name the most direct approach to do your amends, face to face, phone call or letter (i.e., Susan, person in several states away - phone call).

When your list of people and methods are complete, you are ready to start. Writing down the dates you completed an amend is helpful to keep you motivated to finish the entire list. A complete entry might look like this.

JoAnn   Face to face method   Date completed: 12-12-95

Behaviors that support a Step Nine are as follows.

BEHAVIORS		**YES**	**NO**
1.	List of people	_____	_____
2.	Method of contact list	_____	_____
3.	Discussion with sponsor/therapist about those we have questions about contacting	_____	_____
4.	Regular progress	_____	_____
5.	A completed list	_____	_____

EMPOWERMENT
EXERCISE #97

STEP TEN

"Continued to take personal inventory and when we were wrong, promptly admit it."

Continuing to do anything means that you have already started something. Congratulations! You are entering what some call the maintenance part of the Twelve Step Process. Step Ten does not allow you to put secrets into a box that you spent all this time and energy cleaning.

Keeping recovery is a discipline. In this step, doing a daily personal inventory is your daily tool to make sure that you are "staying clean" with yourself and others. In this step, you will reflect daily with yourself and ask, "Is there anything I did today that I know wasn't honest or right?" If so, make an amend to the person who is due this amend.

Those who are married or have children will find a lot of opportunities to practice your recovery and stay humble. This process when integrated, can give you the gift of a life-style of honesty with yourself and integrity with others.

Behaviors that support a Step Ten are:

BEHAVIORS	**YES**	**NO**
1. Daily reflection	_____	_____
2. A way of checking off our findings for the day	_____	_____
3. A way of checking off daily the offense made (remember, "promptly")	_____	_____
4. Discussions about the step with sponsor or therapist	_____	_____

EMPOWERMENT EXERCISE #98

STEP ELEVEN

"Sought through prayer and meditation to improve our conscious contact with God as we understood Him, praying only for the knowledge of His will for us and the power to carry that out."

Prayer has been said to be "talking to God" whether it be requests, petitions, complaints, feelings and whatever other thoughts you might want to share in your personal relationship with God. Meditation is more after you have quieted down some to actually listen to God and hear what is on His mind. Both prayer and meditation are important. You have already established some type of relationship with God. This is just a time to strengthen or improve that relationship.

Asking God for His will may be unfamiliar at first, but as you do it, you will realize His will always has your best interest at heart. He is a father who loves you dearly. Since He takes the time and energy to communicate His will for you, it is my experience that He will give you the Power to carry it out. This may be unfamiliar at first, but this step allows you to practice hearing and following through with God. This can open up a whole new aspect to your spiritual life that will enhance your recovery.

Behaviors that support a Step Eleven are as follows.

BEHAVIORS

		YES	NO
1.	A regular time with God	_____	_____
2.	A way of writing down what God is saying	_____	_____
3.	A way of keeping track of your following God's will and the results	_____	_____
4.	An increased reading or discussing spiritual matters	_____	_____

EMPOWERMENT EXERCISE #99

_____

STEP TWELVE

"Having had a spiritual awakening as a result of these steps, we tried to carry this message to others and to practice these principles in all our affairs."

I enjoy getting results, no matter what the activity or area of my life that I am working on, especially when the results are obvious. This step is such a time. Your recovery has included a lot of hard emotional work and self discovery. It is through these steps that you had a "spiritual awakening."

You now have something to share. There are people throughout your life who will need this message of hope. When these people come across your path, through whatever circumstances, share your strength, hope and experience with them. There are millions of women in relationships with sex addicts and you can believe God will send a few your way if you are at this stage in your recovery.

To be able to practice honesty, integrity, and spirituality is a gift that your recovery has given to you. To keep recovery is to keep practicing what you learned in your steps that have given you recovery.

Behaviors that support Step Twelve are:

BEHAVIOR		**Yes**	**No**
1.	Continued honesty and integrity	_____	_____
2.	Continued amends when they are due	_____	_____
3.	A life-style of relationships	_____	_____

EMPOWERMENT EXERCISE #100

GIVING IT AWAY

In a study of alcoholics who were followed for ten years by a researcher, it was found that there were only two variables that set apart the recovering alcoholic still sober for ten years and the alcoholics who went back to drinking.

Those who stayed sober were regularly attending their 12 Step Support Group, Alcoholic Anonymous, as one of the two variables that separated them from the unsuccessful recovering alcoholics. The second variable was the fact that these recovering alcoholics sponsored people in AA. In a sense they were "giving it away." You will hear in recovery time and time again that, "to keep it, you have to give it away." This is now a scientific fact.

As you recover, you will find great changes occur in your life. Your return to sanity will probably be affecting all areas of your life, spiritual, social and sexual. Giving it away ensures that you keep the gains that you have made. Being a part of others recovering, is a great gift to give to yourself.

APPENDIX

APPENDIX A

FEELINGS EXERCISE

1. I feel (put feeling word here) when (put a present situation when you feel this).
2. I first remember feeling (put the same feeling word here) when (explain earliest occurrence of this feeling).

Abandoned	Battered	Considerate	Distrusted	Goofy
Abused	Beaten	Consumed	Disturbed	Grateful
Aching	Beautiful	Content	Dominated	Greedy
Accepted	Belligerent	Cool	Domineering	Grief
Accused	Belittled	Courageous	Doomed	Grim
Accepting	Bereaved	Courteous	Doubtful	Grimy
Admired	Betrayed	Coy	Dreadful	Grouchy
Adored	Bewildered	Crabby	Eager	Grumpy
Adventurous	Blamed	Cranky	Ecstatic	Hard
Affectionate	Blaming	Crazy	Edgy	Harried
Agony	Bonded	Creative	Edified	Hassled
Alienated	Bored	Critical	Elated	Healthy
Aloof	Bothered	Criticized	Embarrassed	Helpful
Aggravated	Brave	Cross	Empowered	Helpless
Agreeable	Breathless	Crushed	Empty	Hesitant
Aggressive	Bristling	Cuddly	Enraged	High
Alive	Broken-up	Curious	Enraptured	Hollow
Alone	Bruised	Cut	Enthusiastic	Honest
Alluring	Bubbly	Damned	Enticed	Hopeful
Amazed	Burdened	Dangerous	Esteemed	Hopeless
Amused	Burned	Daring	Exasperated	Horrified
Angry	Callous	Dead	Excited	Hostile
Anguished	Calm	Deceived	Exhilarated	Humiliated
Annoyed	Capable	Deceptive	Exposed	Hurried
Anxious	Captivated	Defensive	Fake	Hurt
Apart	Carefree	Delicate	Fascinated	Hyper
Apathetic	Careful	Delighted	Feisty	Ignorant
Apologetic	Careless	Demeaned	Ferocious	Ignored
Appreciated	Caring	Demoralized	Foolish	Immature
Appreciative	Cautious	Dependent	Forced	Impatient
Apprehensive	Certain	Depressed	Forceful	Important
Appropriate	Chased	Deprived	Forgiven	Impotent
Approved	Cheated	Deserted	Forgotten	Impressed
Argumentative	Cheerful	Desirable	Free	Incompetent
Aroused	Childlike	Desired	Friendly	Incomplete
Astonished	Choked-up	Despair	Frightened	Independent
Assertive	Close	Despondent	Frustrated	Insecure
Attached	Cold	Destroyed	Full	Innocent
Attacked	Comfortable	Different	Funny	Insignificant
Attentive	Comforted	Dirty	Furious	Insincere
Attractive	Competent	Disenchanted	Gay	Isolated
Aware	Competitive	Disgusted	Generous	Inspired
Awestruck	Complacent	Disinterested	Gentle	Insulted
Badgered	Complete	Dispirited	Genuine	Interested
Baited	Confident	Distressed	Giddy	Intimate
Bashful	Confused	Distrustful	Giving	Intolerant

Involved	Pleased	Separated	Tormented
Irate	Positive	Sensuous	Torn
Irrational	Powerless	Sexy	Tortured
Irked	Present	Shattered	Touched
Irresponsible	Precious	Shocked	Trapped
Irritable	Pressured	Shot down	Tremendous
Irritated	Pretty	Shy	Tricked
Isolated	Proud	Sickened	Trusted
Jealous	Pulled apart	Silly	Trustful
Jittery	Put down	Sincere	Trusting
Joyous	Puzzled	Sinking	Ugly
Lively	Quarrelsome	Smart	Unacceptable
Lonely	Queer	Smothered	Unapproachable
Loose	Quiet	Smug	Unaware
Lost	Raped	Sneaky	Uncertain
Loving	Ravished	Snowed	Uncomfortable
Low	Ravishing	Soft	Under control
Lucky	Real	Solid	Understanding
Lustful	Refreshed	Solitary	Understood
Mad	Regretful	Sorry	Undesirable
Maudlin	Rejected	Spacey	Unfriendly
Malicious	Rejuvenated	Special	Ungrateful
Mean	Rejecting	Spiteful	Unified
Miserable	Relaxed	Spontaneous	Unhappy
Misunderstood	Relieved	Squelched	Unimpressed
Moody	Remarkable	Starved	Unsafe
Morose	Remembered	Stiff	Unstable
Mournful	Removed	Stimulated	Upset
Mystified	Repulsed	Stifled	Uptight
Nasty	Repulsive	Strangled	Used
Nervous	Resentful	Strong	Useful
Nice	Resistant	Stubborn	Useless
Numb	Responsible	Stuck	Unworthy
Nurtured	Responsive	Stunned	Validated
Nuts	Repressed	Stupid	Valuable
Obsessed	Respected	Subdued	Valued
Offended	Restless	Submissive	Victorious
Open	Revolved	Successful	Violated
Ornery	Riled	Suffocated	Violent
Out of control	Rotten	Sure	Voluptuous
Overcome	Ruined	Sweet	Vulnerable
Overjoyed	Sad	Sympathy	Warm
Overpowered	Safe	Tainted	Wary
Overwhelmed	Satiated	Tearful	Weak
Pampered	Satisfied	Tender	Whipped
Panicked	Scared	Tense	Whole
Paralyzed	Scolded	Terrific	Wicked
Paranoid	Scorned	Terrified	Wild
Patient	Scrutinized	Thrilled	Willing
peaceful	Secure	Ticked	Wiped out
Pensive	Seduced	Tickled	Wishful
Perceptive	Seductive	Tight	Withdrawn
Perturbed	Self-centered	Timid	Wonderful
Phony	Self-conscious	Tired	Worried
Pleasant	Selfish	Tolerant	Worthy

The Twelve Steps of Alcoholics Anonymous

1. We admitted we were powerless over alcohol--that our lives had become unmanageable.

2. Came to believe that a Power greater than ourselves could restore us to sanity.

3. Made a decision to turn our will and our lives over to the care of God as we understood Him.

4. Made a searching and fearless moral inventory of ourselves.

5. Admitted to God, to ourselves, and to another human being the exact nature of our wrongs.

6. Were entirely ready to have God remove all these defects of character.

7. Humbly asked Him to remove our shortcomings.

8. Made a list of all people we had harmed, and became willing to make amends to them all.

9. Made direct amends to such people wherever possible, except when to do so would injure them or others.

10. Continued to take personal inventory, and when we were wrong, promptly admitted it.

11. Sought through prayer and meditation to improve our conscious contact with God as we understood Him, praying only for knowledge of His will for us and the power to carry that out.

12. Having had a spiritual awakening as the result of these steps, we tried to carry this message to others and to practice these principles in all our affairs.

The Twelve Steps reprinted for adaptation by permission of AA World Services, Inc. Copyright 1939.

The Twelve Steps of CO-SA

1. We admitted we were powerless over our co-dependency with the sex addict, and--that our lives had become unmanageable.

2. Came to believe that a Power greater than ourselves could restore us to sanity.

3. Made a decision to turn our will and our lives over to the care of God as we understood Him.

4. Made a searching and fearless moral inventory of ourselves.

5. Admitted to God, to ourselves, and to another human being the exact nature of our wrongs.

6. Were entirely ready to have God remove all these defects of character.

7. Humbly asked Him to remove our shortcomings.

8. Made a list of all people we had harmed, and became willing to make amends to them all.

9. Made direct amends to such people wherever possible, except when to do so would injure them or others.

10. Continued to take personal inventory, and when we were wrong, promptly admitted it.

11. Sought through prayer and meditation to improve our conscious contact with God as we understood Him, praying only for knowledge of His will for us and the power to carry that out.

12. Having had a spiritual awakening as the result of these steps, we tried to carry this message to others and to practice these principles in all our affairs.

APPENDIX C

SUPPORT GROUPS

SEX ADDICTION

Sex Addicts Anonymous (SAA)
P.O. Box 70949
Houston, TX 77270
(713) 869-4902

Sexaholics Anonymous
P.O. Box 111910
Nashville, TN 37222-1910
(615) 331-6901

Sexual Compulsives
Anonymous (SCA)
Old Chelsea Station,
P.O. Box 1585
New York, NY 10013-0935
1-800-977-HEAL

Sex and Love Addicts Anony-
mous (SLAA)
P.O. Box 119, New Town
Branch,
Boston, MA 02258
(617) 332-1845

Sexual Recovery Anonymous
(SRA),
PO Box 73, Planetarium Station,
New York, NY 10024
(212) 340-4650 or:
PO Box 72044
Burnaby, BC V5H4PQ Canada
(604) 290-9382

FOR THE PARTNER OR FAMILY MEMBER

Co-dependents of Sex
Addicts (COSA),
P.O. Box 14537
Minneapolis, MN 55414,
(612) 537-6904

S-Anon International Family
Groups
P.O. Box 111242
Nashville, TN 37222-1242
(615) 833-3152

Co-SLAA
P.O. Box 614
Brookline, MA 02146

Recovering Couples
Anonymous (RCA)
P.O. Box 11872
St. Louis, MO 63105
(314) 830-2600

SEXUAL TRAUMA SURVIVORS

Survivors of Incest Anonymous (SIA)
P.O. Box 21817
Baltimore, MD 21222
(410) 282-3400

Incest Survivors Anonymous
(ISA)
P.O. Box 17245
Long Beach, CA 90807

Sexual Assault Recovery Anony-
mous (SARA Society),
P.O. Box 16
Surrey, British Columbia,
V35 424, Canada
(604) 584-2626

APPENDIX D
MATERIAL DESCRIPTIONS

Now That I Know, What Should I Do?, **by Weiss--$69.95** This 90 minute video answers the ten most frequently asked questions by partners just finding out about their spouse's sexual addiction. The need for counseling is significantly reduced by listening to this video.

Sexual Anorexia, **by Weiss--90 min.Video $69.95** Sexual anorexia paralyzes those from having intimate relationships. This video will provide practical steps to stop withholding behaviors and begin intimacy in present and future relationships.

Women Who Love Sex Addicts, **by Weiss--$14.95** This book discusses what a partner can do to help cope in a relationship with a sex addict. Partners of sex addicts will find this book both informative and comforting.

Beyond Love: 12 Step Recovery Guide for Partners, **by Weiss--$14.95** This is an interactive workbook that allows the partner to gain insight and strength through working the Twelve Steps. This book can be used individually or as a group step-study workbook.

An Affair of the Mind, by Hall--$14.95 This is a woman's story of how she walked through the process of her husband's sex addiction. This book is written from a religious perspective and touches on the partner's pain. I often recommend this book for the sex addict so he can feel and understand the other side of this disease.

Sex, Lies and Forgiveness, **by Schneider--$14.95** This book is dedicated to couple recovery and includes research as well as firsthand accounts from those going through their own recovery as a couple.

How to Love When it Hurts So Bad, **by Weiss-- $38.00** This 4-tape audio series and workbook deals with the partner issues of an addict. This has a religious focus and gives biblical answers to boundaries, tough love, and how to love an addict the way God does.

Pathways To Intimacy, by Weiss Robison, Evans--$35.00/5 Audios This audio series presents solutions to gaining intimacy in the marriage relationship. Nuggets of information are gleaned from national television host James Robison author Douglas Weiss, Ph.D. and Debra Evans. This is a great road map for couples wanting more out of their relationship.

Good Enough to Wait--by Weiss--$39.95 This 60 minute video is the Christian sex talk for teenagers for the 21st Century. Dr. Weiss combines the best scriptural teaching with a decade of research in the field of sexuality. This video comes with a commitment card (which researchers have found to profoundly increase the chances of waiting till marriage) and booklet. Youth Pastors in addition to parents will also greatly benefit from this video presentation.

She Has A Secret, by Weiss--Book $14.95 This book combines true stories of female sex addicts along with the most recent research on female sex addiction and understanding it.

The Final Freedom: Pioneering Sexual Addiction Recovery, **by Weiss--Audio $35.00/Book $22.95** This five-audio-tape series/book gives more current information than many professional counselors have today. In addition to informing sex addicts and their partners about sex addiction, it gives hope for recovery. The information provided in this product would cost hundreds of dollars in counseling hours to receive. Many have attested to successful recovery from this product alone.

101 Practical Exercises for Sexual Addiction Recovery, **by Weiss--$39.95** This workbook contains 101 proven techniques that Dr. Weiss has used to successfully help thousands obtain and maintain their sex addiction recovery. This is a great follow up tool for *The Final Freedom*.

101 Freedom Exercises: A Christian Guide for Sex Addiction Recovery, **by Weiss--$39.95** (Christian version of *101 Practical Exercises*)

Steps of Hope: 12 Step Recovery Guide for Sex Addiction, **by Weiss--$14.95** This is a thorough interaction with the Twelve Steps of recovery. This workbook can be used in Twelve Step study groups, or individually.

Steps to Freedom: A Christian 12 Step Guide, **by Weiss--$14.95** (Christian version of *Steps of Hope*.)

ORDER FORM

ITEM	QUAN	PRICE	TOTAL

VIDEOS/AUDIOS

video/audio

The Final Freedom, (5 audios) by Weiss _____ $ 35.00 _____
Now That I Know, What Should I Do?, by Weiss (90 min Video) _____ 69.95 _____
How To Love When It Hurts So Bad, (4 audios/1 wkbk) by Weiss _____ 38.00 _____
Sexual Anorexia, (90 min Video) by Weiss _____ 69.95 _____
Good Enough To Wait, (1hr. Video) by Weiss _____ 39.95 _____
Pathways To Intimacy, (Audio Series) _____ 35.00 _____

BOOKS/WORKBOOKS

The Final Freedom, (Book) by Weiss _____ $ 22.95 _____
She Has A Secret, by Weiss _____ 14.95 _____
*101 **Practical** Exercises for Sex Addiction Recovery*, by Weiss _____ 39.95 _____
*101 **Freedom** Exercises for Sex Addiction Recovery*, by Weiss _____ 39.95 _____
Partner's Recovery Guide: 100 Empowering Exercises, by Weiss _____ 39.95 _____
Beyond Love, by Weiss _____ 14.95 _____
Steps of Hope, by Weiss _____ 14.95 _____
Steps to Freedom, by Weiss _____ 14.95
Women Who Love Sex Addicts, by Weiss & DeBusk _____ 14.95 _____
Affair of the Mind, by Hall _____ 14.95 _____
Out of the Shadows, by Carnes _____ 14.95 _____
Faithful and True, by Laaser _____ 14.95 _____
Hope and Recovery, by Hazelden _____ 14.95 _____
Sex, Lies and Forgiveness, by Schneider _____ 14.95 _____
She Has A Secret, by Weiss _____ 14.95 _____

Sub Total _____
8.25% Sales Tax (in Texas only) _____
Shipping/Handling-add $3 + .50 for each additional item (in USA) _____
Shipping/Handling-add $6 + $1 for each additional item (outside USA) _____
Total

To order: 817-377-4278

VISA/MC/DISCOVER #_____ EXP DATE _____

NAME _____ SIGNATURE _____

ADDRESS _____ CITY _____

STATE _____ ZIP CODE _____ PHONE (_____)_____

OR MAIL TO: Heart to Heart Counseling Centers, P.O. Box 16716, Fort Worth, TX, 76162-0716
OR E-MAIL TO: www.sexaddict.com   or   heart2heart@xc.org
(Make Checks payable to Heart to Heart Counseling Centers)

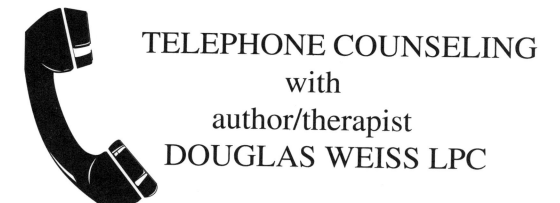

TELEPHONE COUNSELING
with
author/therapist
DOUGLAS WEISS LPC

Dear Reader,

We are happy to introduce you to the opportunity of telephone counseling with Douglas Weiss at Heart to Heart Counseling Centers. Counseling is provided for those having issues with sexual addiction, sexual co-addiction, victims of sexual trauma, marriage and family issues and various emotional disorders. As you work through the *Partner's Recovery Guide*, and you have some concerns or issues you would like professional help with, call Heart to Heart Counseling Centers. All telephone counseling is strictly confidential.

To schedule a telephone appointment with Douglas Weiss, **call 817-377-4278**. Appointments are available Monday - Wednesday 8:00 a.m. to 8:00 p.m. central time. When you call to schedule your appointment, you will be given a **toll-free number** (within USA). Call the toll-free number at the time of your scheduled appointment. We will need 24 hours notice for changes in appointments or cancellations otherwise you will be billed for your appointment.

Counseling costs are $125.00 per hour. We accept Mastercard, VISA, or Discover, American Express or you may send a check in advance of your scheduled appointment. We look forward to hearing from you.

VIDEO THERAPY
& Education

By Douglas Weiss, Ph.D.

Dr. Weiss has put together his valuable
sex addiction therapy & education
into 6 NEW videos!

Video Session #1: **How Did I get This Way? (90 Min)**

Video Session #2: **How To Get and Stay Clean**

Video Session #3: **Sexual Abuse: Living Beyond the Pain**

Video Session #4: **Dealing with Family of Origin Issues**

Video Session #5: **Guilt and Shame**

Video Session #6: **The Christian Sex Addict**

Why Video Therapy?

❑   Is it hard to find a local therapist who understands sex addiction?

❑   Do you want help now without waiting for an appointment?

❑   Would you like the confidentiality of counseling in the privacy of your home?

❑   Are you uncomfortable talking to a therapist about your sex addiction?

❑   Where can you get counseling by a national expert for these prices?

The most affordable way to get this much information!

3-DAY INTENSIVE SCHEDULE
for 2000
with Douglas Weiss, Ph.D.
Fort Worth, Texas

Our 3-Day Intensive workshops are a huge success. Couples receive 3 sessions (individuals 2 sessions) per day of personal counseling with Dr. Weiss. Support groups are available during the evening. The following are 2000 Intensive dates available.

Individual Intensive Dates

Jan 3-5	July 17-19
Jan 17-19	July 31-Aug 2
Jan 31-Feb 2	Aug 14-16
Feb 14-16	Sept 4-6
Feb 28-Mar 1	Sept 18-20
Mar 13-15	Oct 2-4
April 3-5	Oct 16-18
April 17-19	Nov 6-8
May 1-3	Nov 20-22
May 15-17	Dec 4-6
June 5-7	Dec 18-20
June 19-21	

Couple Intensive Dates

Jan 10-12	July 10-12
Jan 24-26	July 24-26
Feb 7-9	Aug 7-9
Feb 21-23	Aug 21-23
Mar 6-8	Sept 11-13
Mar 20-22	Sept 25-27
April 10-12	Oct 9-11
April 24-26	Oct 23-25
May 8-10	Nov 13-15
May 22-24	Nov 27-29
June 12-14	Dec 11-13

Cost: $950/Individual Pre-paid*
        $1,200/Couple Pre-paid*

(MC, Visa, Discover, & American Express accepted)
*Does not include travel, hotel, or food

RESEARCH AND MEDIA OPPORTUNITY

The future of the recovery movement depends on people like you. The research we started must continue. If you would like to be a part of future research surveys for furthering the study of recovery, please help us by filling in the information below.

The media is opening its doors to understanding sexual addiction. They want real people with real struggles. If you have an interest in discussing recovery and sharing your story along with others, please fill out the information below and fax, e-mail, or mail it to the address below.

I am interested in being a part of future:

❑   research opportunities.
❑   media opportunities (usually TV).
❑   print or radio opportunities

Name (first name only is okay) _____

Address _____

Phone _____

E-Mail Address _____

Heart to Heart Counseling Center
P.O. Box 16716
Fort Worth, TX 76162
Heart2Heart@xc.org
(817) 377-4278
(817) 335-3841 (fax)
www.sexaddict.com